Prayer: The Great Means of Salvation and of Perfection

Prayer
The Great Means of Salvation and of Perfection

Excerpt (Part 1)

❧

St Alphonsus Maria de Liguori

Edited by the Rev. Eugene Grimm CSSR

Cana Press

APPROBATION

By virtue of the authority granted me by the Most Rev. Nicholas Mauron, Superior General of the Congregation of the Most Holy Redeemer, I hereby sanction the publication of the work entitled "The Great Means of Salvation and of Perfection," which is Vol. III. of the new and complete edition in English of the works of Saint Alphonsus de Liguori, called "The Centenary Edition."

ELIAS FRED. SCHAUER,
Sup. Prov. Baltimorensis.
BALTIMORE, MD., April 26, 1886.

First Published by
Benziger Brothers
New York, Cincinnati, & St. Louis

Newly revised and edited
Cana Press © 2020

All rights reserved

For information, address:
PO Box 85
Colebrook,
Tasmania, 7027,
Australia

notredamemonastery.org

ISBN
978-0-6488688-3-5

To the Incarnate Word

The Beloved of the Eternal Father,
The Blessed of the Lord,
The Author of Life,
The King of Glory,
The Saviour of the World,
The Expected of Nations,
The Desire of the Eternal Hills,
The Bread of Heaven,
The Mediator between God and Man,
The Master of Virtues,
The Lamb without Spot,
The Man of Sorrows,
The Eternal Priest,
The Victim of Love,
The Home of Sinners,
The Fountain of Graces,
The Good Shepherd,
The Lover of Souls,

Alphonsus the Sinner
Consecrates this Book.

Dedication to Jesus and Mary

O INCARNATE WORD, Thou hast given Thy Blood and Thy Life to confer on our prayers that power by which, according to Thy promise, they obtain for us all that we ask. And we, O God, are so careless of our salvation, that we will not even ask Thee for the graces that we must have if we should be saved! In prayer Thou hast given us the key of all Thy Divine treasures; and we, rather than pray, choose to remain in our misery. Alas! O Lord, enlighten us, and make us know the value of prayers, offered in Thy name and by Thy merits, in the eyes of Thy Eternal Father. I consecrate to Thee this my book; bless it, and grant that all those into whose hands it falls may have the will to pray always, and may exert themselves to stir up others also to avail themselves of this great means of salvation.

To thee also do I recommend my little work, O Mary, great Mother of God: patronise it, and obtain for all who read it the spirit of prayer, and of continual recourse in all their necessities to thy Son, and to thee, who art the Dispenser of graces, the Mother of mercy, and who never leavest unsatisfied him who recommends himself to thee, O mighty Virgin, but obtainest from God for thy servants whatever thou askest.

CONTENTS

Preface ... 1
Definition of Prayer ... 3
Plan of the Work ... 4

Chapter 1
The Necessity of Prayer

Prayer is a Means Necessary to Salvation ... 5
Without Prayer It is Impossible to Resist Temptations
  and to Keep the Commandments ... 9
Invocation of the Saints ... 14
  1. Is it good and useful to have recourse to the intercession of the saints? ... 14
  2. Is it good to invoke also the souls in Purgatory? ... 15
  3. It is our duty to pray for the souls in Purgatory ... 17
  4. Is it necessary to invoke the Saints? ... 21
The Intercession of the Blessed Virgin ... 23
Conclusion of the Chapter ... 27

Chapter 2
The Power of Prayer

Excellence of Prayer and its Power with God ... 29
Power of Prayer against Temptation ... 31
God is Always Ready to Hear Us ... 34
We Should not Limit Ourselves to Asking for Little Things:
  to Pray is Better than to Meditate ... 38
Conclusion of the Chapter ... 42

Chapter 3
The Conditions of Prayer

Which are the Requisite Conditions	45
Object of Prayer	45
Can we pray efficaciously for others?	46
We ought to pray for sinners	47
We must ask for the graces necessary to salvation	49
Other conditions of prayer	51
The Humility with which we Should Pray	51
The Confidence with which we Should Pray	57
Excellence and necessity of this virtue	57
Foundation of our confidence	61
The prayer of sinners	65
The Perseverance Required in Prayer	71
Why God delays granting us final perseverance.	
Conclusion.	75

Preface

I have published several spiritual works,—on Visiting the Blessed Sacrament, on the Passion of Jesus Christ, on the Glories of Mary, and, besides, a work against the Materialists and Deists, with other devout little treatises. Lately I brought out a work on the Infancy of our Saviour, entitled Novena for Christmas; and another entitled Preparation for Death, besides the one on the Eternal Maxims, most useful for meditation and for sermons, to which are added nine discourses suitable during seasons of Divine chastisements. But I do not think that I have written a more useful work than the present, in which I speak of prayer as a necessary and certain means of obtaining salvation, and all the graces that we require for that object. If it were in my power, I would distribute a copy of it to every Catholic in the world, in order to show him the absolute necessity of prayer for salvation.

I say this, because, on the one hand, I see that the absolute necessity of prayer is taught throughout the Holy Scriptures, and by all the holy Fathers; while, on the other hand, I see that Christians are very careless in their practice of this great means of salvation. And, sadder still, I see that preachers take very little care to speak of it to their flocks, and confessors to their penitents; I see, moreover, that even the spiritual books now popular do not speak sufficiently of it; for there is not a thing preachers, and confessors, and spiritual books should insist upon with more warmth and energy than prayer; not but that they teach many excellent means of keeping ourselves in the grace of God, such as avoiding the occasions of sin, frequenting the sacraments, resisting temptations, hearing the Word of God, meditating on the eternal truths, and other means,—all of them, I admit, most useful; but, I say, what profit is there in sermons, meditations, and all the other means pointed out by masters of the spiritual life, if we forget to pray? since our Lord has declared that He will grant His graces to no one who does not pray. "Ask and ye shall receive" (*John 16: 24*).

Without prayer, in the ordinary course of Providence, all the meditations that we make, all our resolutions, all our promises, will be useless. If we do not pray, we shall always be unfaithful to the inspirations of God, and to the promises we made to Him. Because, in order actually to do good, to conquer temptations, to practice virtues, and to observe God's law, it is not enough to receive illumination from God, and to meditate and make resolutions, but we require, moreover, the actual assistance of God; and, as we shall soon see, He does not give this assistance except to those who pray, and pray with perseverance.

The light we receive, and the considerations and good resolutions that we make, are of use to incite us to the act of prayer when we are in danger and are tempted to transgress God's law; for then prayer will obtain for us God's help, and we shall be preserved from sin; but if in such moments we do not pray, we shall be lost.

My intention in prefacing my book with this sentiment is, that my readers may thank God for giving them an opportunity, by means of this little book, to receive the grace of reflecting more deeply on the importance of prayer; for all adults who are saved, are ordinarily saved by this single means of grace. And therefore I ask my readers to thank God; for surely it is a great mercy when he gives the light and the grace to pray.

I hope, then, that you, my beloved brother, after reading this little work, will never from this day forward neglect to have continual recourse to God in prayer, whenever you are tempted to offend Him. If ever in times past you have had your conscience burdened with many sins, know that the cause of this has been the neglect of prayer, and not asking God for help to resist the temptations that assailed you.

I pray you, therefore, to read it again and again with the greatest attention; not because it is my production, but because it is a means that God offers you for the good of your eternal salvation, thereby giving you to understand that He wishes you to be saved. And after having read it yourself, induce as many of your friends and neighbours as you can to read it also. Now let us begin in the name of the Lord.

Definition of Prayer

The Apostle writes to Timothy: "Beseech, therefore, that first of all supplications, petitions, and thanksgivings be made" (*1 Tim. 2: 1*). St. Thomas explains that prayer is properly the lifting up of the soul to God (*2. 2. q. 83, a. 17*). Petition is that kind of prayer which begs for determinate objects; when the thing sought is indeterminate (as when we say, "Incline to my aid, O God!") it is called supplication. Obsecration is a solemn adjuration, or representation of the grounds on which we dare to ask a favour; as when we say, "By Thy Cross and Passion, O Lord, deliver us!" Finally, thanksgiving is the returning of thanks for benefits received, whereby, says St. Thomas, we merit to receive greater favours. Prayer, in a strict sense, says the holy Doctor, means recourse to God; but in its general signification it includes all the kinds just enumerated. It is in this latter sense that the word is used in this book.

Plan of the Work

In order, then, to attach ourselves to this great means of salvation, we must first of all consider how necessary it is to us, and how powerful it is to obtain for us all the graces that we can desire from God, if we know how to ask for them as we ought. Hence, in the first part, we will speak first of the necessity and power of prayer; and next, of the conditions necessary to make it efficacious with God. Then, in the second part, we will show that the grace of prayer is given to all; and there we will treat of the manner in which grace ordinarily operates.

Chapter 1

The Necessity of Prayer

I
Prayer is a Means Necessary to Salvation

One of the errors of Pelagianism was the assertion that prayer is not necessary for salvation. Pelagius, the impious author of that heresy, said that man will only be damned for neglecting to know the truths necessary to be learned. How astonishing! St. Augustine said: "Pelagius discussed everything except how to pray" (*De Nat. et Grat. c. 17*), though, as the Saint held and taught, prayer is the only means of acquiring the science of the Saints; according to the text of St. James: "If any man wants wisdom, let him ask of God, Who giveth to all abundantly, and upbraideth not" (*James 1: 5*).

The Scriptures are clear enough in pointing out how necessary it is to pray, if we would be saved. "We ought always to pray, and not to faint" (*Luke 18: 1*). "Watch and pray, that ye enter not into temptation" (*Matt. 26: 41*). "Ask, and it shall be given you" (*Matt. 7: 7*). The words "we ought," "pray," "ask," according to the general consent of theologians, impose the precept, and denote the necessity of prayer.

Wickliffe said that these texts are to be understood, not precisely of prayer, but only of the necessity of good works, for in his system prayer was only well-doing; but this was his error, and was expressly condemned by the Church. Hence Lessius wrote that it is heresy to deny that prayer is necessary for salvation in adults, as it evidently appears from Scripture that prayer is the means, without which we cannot obtain the help necessary for salvation (*De just. lib. 2. c. 38, d. 3*).

The reason of this is evident. Without the assistance of God's grace we can do no good thing: "Without Me, ye can do nothing" (*John 15: 5*). St. Augustine remarks on this passage that our Lord did not say, "Without Me, ye can complete nothing," but "without Me, ye can do nothing"; giving us to understand, that without grace we cannot even begin to do a good thing. Nay more, St. Paul writes, that of ourselves we cannot even have the wish to do good. "Not that we are sufficient to think anything of ourselves, but our sufficiency is from God" (*2 Cor. 3: 5*). If we cannot even think a good thing, much less can we wish it.

The same thing is taught in many other passages of Scripture: "God worketh all in all" (*1 Cor 12:6*). "I will cause you to walk in My commandments, and to keep My judgments, and do them" (*Ezek. 37: 27*). So that, as St. Leo I says, "Man does no good thing, except that which God, by His grace, enables him to do," and hence the Council of Trent says: "If anyone shall assert, that without the previous inspiration of the Holy Ghost, and His assistance, man can believe, hope, love, or repent, as he ought, in order to obtain the grace of justification, let him be anathema" (*Sess. 6, Can. 3*).

The author of the Opus Imperfectum says, that God has given to some animals swiftness, to others claws, to other wings, for the preservation of their life; but He has so formed man, that God Himself is his only strength" (*Hom. 18*). So that man is completely unable to provide for his own safety, since God has willed that whatever he has, or can have, should come entirely from the assistance of His grace.

But this grace is not given in God's ordinary Providence, except to those who pray for it; according to the celebrated saying of Gennadius. "We believe that no one approaches to be saved, except by the help of God; that no one merits this help, unless he prays."

From these two premises, on the one hand, that we can do nothing without the assistance of grace; and on the other, that this assistance is only given ordinarily by God to the man that prays, who does not see that the consequence follows that prayer is absolutely necessary to us for salvation? And although the first graces that come to us without any co-operation on our part, such as the call to faith or to penance, are, as St. Augustine says, granted by God even to those who do not pray, yet the Saint considers it certain that the other graces, and specially the grace of perseverance, are not granted except in answer to prayer: "God gives us some things, as the beginning of faith, even when we do not pray. Other things, such as perseverance, he has only provided for those who pray."

Hence it is that the generality of theologians, following St. Basil, St. Chrysostom, Clement of Alexandria, St. Augustine, and other Fathers, teach that prayer is necessary to adults, not only because of the obligation of the precept (as they say), but because it is necessary as a means of salvation. That is to say, in the ordinary course of Providence, it is impossible that a Christian should be saved without recommending himself to God and asking for the graces necessary to salvation. St. Thomas teaches the same: "After Baptism, continual prayer is necessary to man, in order that he may enter Heaven; for though by Baptism our sins are remitted, there still remain concupiscence to assail us from within, and the world and the devil to assail us from without" (*P. 3, q. 39, a. 5*).

The reason then which makes us certain of the necessity of prayer is shortly this: in order to be saved we must contend and conquer: "He that striveth for the mastery is not crowned except he strive lawfully" (*2 Tim. 2: 5*). But without the Divine assistance we cannot resist the might of so many and so powerful enemies: now this assistance is only granted through prayer; therefore without prayer there is no salvation.

Moreover, that prayer is the only ordinary means of receiving the Divine gifts is more distinctly proved by St. Thomas in another place, where he says, that whatever graces God has from all eternity determined to give us, He will only give them if we pray for them. St. Gregory says the same thing: "Man by prayer merits to receive that which God had from all eternity determined to give him." Not, says St. Thomas, that prayer is necessary in order that God may know our necessities, but in order that we may know the necessity of having recourse to God to obtain the help necessary for our salvation, and may thus acknowledge Him to be the author of all our good. As, therefore, it is God's law that we should provide ourselves with bread by sowing corn, and with wine by planting vines; so has He ordained that we should receive the graces necessary to salvation by means of prayer: "Ask, and it shall be given you; seek, and ye shall find" (*Matt. 7: 7*).

We, in a word, are merely beggars, who have nothing but what God bestows on us as alms: "But I am a beggar and poor" (*Ps. 39: 18*). The Lord, says St. Augustine, desires and wills to pour forth his graces upon us, but will not give them except to him who prays. "God wishes to give, but only gives to him who asks." This is declared in the words, "Seek and it shall be given to you." Whence it follows, says St. Teresa, that he who seeks not, does not receive. As moisture is necessary for the life of plants to prevent them from drying up, so, says St. Chrysostom, is prayer necessary for our salvation. Or, as he says in another place, prayer vivifies the soul, as the soul vivifies the body: "As the body without the soul cannot live, so the soul without prayer is dead and emits an offensive odour."

He uses these words, because the man who omits to recommend himself to God, at once begins to be defiled with sins. Prayer is also called the food of the soul, because the body cannot be supported without food; nor can the soul, says St. Augustine, be kept alive without prayer: "As the flesh is nourished by food, so is man supported by prayers."

All these comparisons used by the holy Fathers are intended by them to teach the absolute necessity of prayer for the salvation of everyone.

2

Without Prayer It is Impossible to Resist Temptations and to Keep the Commandments

Moreover, prayer is the most necessary weapon of defence against our enemies; he who does not avail himself of it, says St. Thomas, is lost. He does not doubt that the reason of Adam's fall was because he did not recommend himself to God when he was tempted: "He sinned because he had not recourse to the Divine assistance" (*P. 1, q. 94, a. 4*). St. Gelasius says the same of the rebel angels: "Receiving the grace of God in vain, they could not persevere, because they did not pray."

St. Charles Borromeo, in a pastoral letter, observes that among all the means of salvation recommended by Jesus Christ in the Gospel, the first place is given to prayer; and he has determined that this should distinguish his Church from all false religions, when he calls her "the house of prayer": "My house is a house of prayer" (*Matt. 21: 13*). St. Charles concludes that prayer is the beginning and progress and the completion of all virtues." So that in darkness, distress, and danger, we have no other hope than to raise our eyes to God, and with fervent prayers to beseech His mercy to save us: "As we know not," said king Josaphat, "what to do, we can only turn our eyes to Thee" (*2 Par. 20: 12*).

This also was David's practice, who could find no other means of safety from his enemies, than continual prayer to God to deliver him from their snares: "My eyes are ever towards the Lord; for He shall pluck my feet out of the snare" (*Ps. 24: 16*). So he did nothing but pray: "Look Thou upon me, and have mercy on me; for I am alone and poor. I cried unto Thee, a Lord; save me that I may keep Thy Commandments" (*Ps. 118: 146*). Lord, turn Thine eyes to me, have pity on me, and save me; for I can do nothing, and beside Thee there is none that can help me.

And, indeed how could we ever resist our enemies and observe God's precepts, especially since Adam's sin, which has rendered us so weak and infirm, unless we had prayer as a means whereby we can obtain from God sufficient light and strength to enable us to observe them? It was a blasphemy of Luther's to say that after the sin of Adam the observance of God's law has become absolutely impossible to man. Jansenius also said that there are some precepts which are impossible even to the just, with the power which they actually have, and so far his proposition bears a good sense; but it was justly condemned by the Church for the addition he made to it, when he said that they have not the grace to make the precepts possible.

It is true, says St. Augustine, that man, in consequence of his weakness, is unable to fulfill some of God's commands with his present strength and the ordinary grace given to all men; but he can easily, by prayer, obtain such further aid as he requires for his salvation: "God commands not impossibilities, but by commanding he suggests to you to do what you can, to ask for what is beyond your strength; and He helps you, that you may be able." This is a celebrated text, which was afterwards adopted and made a doctrine of faith by the Council of Trent (*Sess. 6, c. 11*). The holy Doctor immediately adds, "Let us see whence?" (i.e., how man is enabled to do that which he cannot). "By medicine he can do that which his natural weakness renders impossible to him" (*De Nat. et Gr. c. 43*). That is, by prayer we may obtain a remedy for our weakness; for when we pray, God gives us strength to do that which we cannot do of ourselves.

We cannot believe, continues St. Augustine, that God would have imposed on us the observance of a law, and then made the law impossible. When, therefore, God shows us that of ourselves we are unable to observe all His commands it is simply to admonish us to do the easier things by means of the ordinary grace which He bestows on us, and then to do the more difficult things by means of the greater help which we can obtain by prayer. "By the very fact that it is absurd to suppose that God could have commanded us to do impossible things, we are admonished what to do in easy matters, and what to ask for in difficulties" (*De Nat. et Gr. c. 69*).

But why, it will be asked, has God commanded us to do things impossible to our natural strength? Precisely for this, says St. Augustine, that we may be incited to pray for help to do that which of ourselves we cannot do. "He commands some things which we cannot do, that we may know what we ought to ask of him" (*De Gr. et Lib. Arb. c. 16*). And in another place: "The law was given, that grace might be sought for;

grace was given that the law might be fulfilled" (*De Spir. et Litt. c. 19*). The law cannot be kept without grace, and God has given the law with this object, that we may always ask him for grace to observe it. In another place he says: "The law is good, if it be used lawfully; what then, is the lawful use of the law?" He answers: "When by the law we perceive our own weakness, and ask of God the grace to heal us" (*Serm. 156, Ed. Ben.*). St. Augustine then says: We ought to use the law; but for what purpose? To learn by means of the law, which we find to be above our strength, our own inability to observe it, in order that we may then obtain by prayer the Divine aid to cure our weakness.

St. Bernard's teaching is the same: "What are we, or what is our strength, that we should be able to resist so many temptations? This certainly it was that God intended; that we, seeing our deficiencies, and that we have no other help, should with all humility have recourse to his mercy" (*In Quad. 5. 5*). God knows how useful it is to us to be obliged to pray, in order to keep us humble, and to exercise our confidence; and He therefore permits us to be assaulted by enemies too mighty to be overcome by our own strength, that by prayer we may obtain from His mercy aid to resist them; and it is especially to be remarked, that no one can resist the impure temptations of the flesh, without recommending himself to God when he is tempted.

This foe is so terrible that, when it fights with us, it, as it were, takes away all light; it makes us forget all our meditations, all our good resolutions; it makes us also disregard the truths of faith, and even almost lose the fear of the Divine punishments. For it conspires with our natural inclinations, which drive us with the greatest violence to the indulgence of sensual pleasures, that he who in such a moment does not have recourse to God is lost. The only defence against this temptation is prayer, as St. Gregory of Nyssa says: "Prayer is the bulwark of chastity;" and before him Solomon: "And as I knew that I could not otherwise be continent except God gave it, I went to the Lord and besought Him" (*Wisd. 8: 21*). Chastity is a virtue which we have not strength to practice, unless God gives it us; and God does not give this strength except to him who asks for it. But whoever prays for it will certainly obtain it.

Hence St. Thomas observes (in contradiction to Jansenius), that we ought not to say that the precept of chastity, or any other, is impossible to us; for though we cannot observe it by our own strength, we can by God's assistance. "We must say, that what we can do with the Divine assistance is not altogether impossible to us" (*1. 2. q. 109, a. 4*). Nor let it be said that it appears an injustice to order a cripple to walk straight. No, says St. Augustine, it is not an injustice, provided always means are given him to find the remedy for his lameness; for after this, if he continues to go crooked, the fault is his own. "It is most wisely commanded that man should walk uprightly, so that when he sees that he cannot do so of himself, he may seek a remedy to heal the lameness of sin" (*De Perf. Just. hom. c. 3*). Finally, the same holy Doctor says, that he will not know how to live well who does not know how to pray well. "He knows how to live aright who knows how to pray aright" (*Ser. 55, E.B. app.*); and, on the other hand, St. Francis of Assisi says, that without prayer you can never hope to find good fruit in a soul.

Wrongly, therefore, do those sinners excuse themselves who say that they have no strength to resist temptation. But if you have not this strength, why do you not ask for it? is the reproof which St. James gives them: "You have it not, because you ask it not" (*James 4: 2*).

There is no doubt that we are too weak to resist the attacks of our enemies. But, on the other hand, it is certain that God is faithful, as the Apostle says, and will not permit us to be tempted beyond our strength: "God is faithful, who will not suffer you to be tempted above that which you are able; but will make also with the temptation issue, that ye may be able to bear it" (*1 Cor. 10: 13*). "He will provide an issue for it," says Primasius, "by the protection of His grace, that you may be able to withstand the temptation."

We are weak, but God is strong; when we ask Him for aid, He communicates His strength to us; and we shall be able to do all things, as the Apostle reasonably assured himself: "I can do all things in Him who strengtheneth me" (*Phil. 4: 13*). He, therefore, who falls has no excuse (says St. Chrysostom), because he has neglected to pray; for if he had prayed, he would not have been overcome by his enemies. "Nor can anyone be excused who, by ceasing to pray, has shown that he did not wish to overcome his enemy."

3
Invocation of the Saints

1. Is it good and useful to have recourse to the intercession of the saints?

Here a question arises, whether it is necessary to have recourse also to the intercession of the Saints to obtain the grace of God.

That it is a lawful and useful thing to invoke the Saints, as intercessors, to obtain for us, by the merits of Jesus Christ, that which we, by our demerits, are not worthy to receive, is a doctrine of the Church, declared by the Council of Trent. "It is good and useful to invoke them by supplication, and to fly to their aid and assistance to obtain benefits from God through his Son Jesus Christ" (*Sess. 25, De. inv. Sanct.*).

Such innovation was condemned by the impious Calvin, but most illogically. For if it is lawful and profitable to invoke living Saints to aid us, and to beseech them to assist us in prayers, as the Prophet Baruch did: "And pray ye for us to the Lord our God" (*Bar. 1: 13*), and St. Paul: "Brethren, pray for us" (*1 Thess. 5: 25*), and as God Himself commanded the friends of Job to recommend themselves to his prayers, that by the merits of Job he might look favourably on them: "Go to my servant Job, ... and my servant Job shall pray for you; his face I will accept" (*Job 42: 8*); if, then it is lawful to recommend ourselves to the living, how can it be unlawful to invoke the Saints who in Heaven enjoy God face to face?

This is not derogatory to the honour due to God, but it is doubling it; for it is honouring the king not only in His Person but in His servants. Therefore, says St. Thomas, it is good to have recourse to many Saints, "because by the prayers of many we can sometimes obtain that which we cannot by the prayers of one." And if any one object, "But why have recourse to the Saints to pray for us, when they are already praying for all who are worthy of it?" the same Doctor answers, that no one can be said to be worthy that the Saints should pray for him; but that "he becomes worthy by having recourse to the Saint with devotion" (*In 4. Sent. d. 45, q. 3, a. 2*).

2. *Is it good to invoke also the souls in Purgatory?*

Again, it is disputed whether there is any use in recommending one's self to the Souls in Purgatory. Some say that the Souls in that state cannot pray for us; and these rely on the authority of St. Thomas, who says that those Souls, while they are being purified by pain, are inferior to us, and therefore are not in a state to pray for us, but rather require our prayers (*2. 2. q. 83, a. 2*). But many other Doctors, as Bellarmine (*De Purg. 1. 2. c. 15*), Sylvius (*In Suppl. q. 71, a. 6*), Cardinal Gotti (*De St. an. p. vit. q. 4, d. 2*), Lessius (*De Just. 1. 2, c. 37, d. 5*), Medina and others, affirm with great probability, that we should piously believe that God manifests our prayer to those holy souls, in order that they may pray for us; and that so the charitable interchange of mutual prayer may be kept up between them and us.

Nor do St. Thomas' words present much difficulty; for, as Sylvius and Gotti say, it is one thing not to be in a state to pray, another not to be able to pray. It is true that those souls are not in a state to pray, because, as St. Thomas says, while suffering they are inferior to us, and rather require our prayers; nevertheless, in this state they are well able to pray, as they are friends of God. If a father keeps a son whom he tenderly loves in confinement for some fault, and if the son then is not in a state to pray for himself, is that any reason why he cannot pray for others, and may he not expect to obtain what he asks, knowing, as he does, his father's affection for him? So the Souls in Purgatory, being beloved by God, and confirmed in grace, have absolutely no impediment to prevent them from praying for us.

Still the Church does not invoke them, or implore their intercession, because ordinarily they have no cognizance of our prayers. But we may piously believe that God makes our prayers known to them; and then they, full of charity as they are, most assuredly do not omit to pray for us.

St. Catherine of Bologna, whenever she desired any favour, had recourse to the Souls in Purgatory, and was immediately heard. She even testified that by the intercession of the Souls in Purgatory she had obtained many graces which she had not been able to obtain by the intercession of the Saints.

3. It is our duty to pray for the souls in Purgatory

But here let me make a digression in favour of those Holy Souls. If we desire the aid of their prayers, it is but fair that we should mind to aid them with our prayers and good works. I said it is fair, but I should have said it is a Christian duty; for charity obliges us to succour our neighbour when he requires our aid, and we can help him without grievous inconvenience. Now it is certain that amongst our neighbours are to be reckoned the Souls in Purgatory, who, although no longer living in this world, yet have not left the Communion of Saints. "The Souls of the pious dead," says St. Augustine, "are not separated from the Church" (*De Civitate Dei. 1. 20, c. 9*), and St. Thomas says more to our purpose that the charity which is due to the dead who died in the grace of God is only an extension of the same charity which we owe to our neighbour while living: "Charity, which is the bond which unites the member of the Church, extends not only to the living, but also to the dead who die in charity" (*In 4. Sent. d. 45, q. 2, s. 2*).

Therefore, we ought to succour, according to our ability, those holy souls as our neighbours; and as their necessities are greater than those of our other neighbours, for this reason our duty to succour them seems also to be greater.

But now, what are the necessities of those holy prisoners? It is certain that their pains are immense. The fire that tortures them, says St. Augustine, is more excruciating than any pain that man can endure in this life: "That fire will be more painful than anything that man can suffer in this life" (*In Ps. 37*). St. Thomas thinks the same, and supposes it to be identical with the fire of Hell: "The damned are tormented and the elect purified in the same fire" (*In 4. Sent. d. 21, q. 1, a. 1*). And this only relates to the pains of sense.

But the pain of loss (that is, the privation of the sight of God), which those Holy Souls suffer, is much greater; because not only their natural affection, but also the supernatural love of God, wherewith they burn, draws them with such violence to be united with their Sovereign Good, that when they see the barrier which their sins have put in the way, they feel a pain so acute, that if they were capable of death, they could not live a moment. So that, as St. Chrysostom says, this pain of the deprivation of God tortures them incomparably more than the pain of sense: "The flames of a thousand Hells together could not inflict much torments as the pain of loss by itself." So that those Holy Souls would rather suffer every other possible torture than be deprived for a single instant of the union with God for which they long.

So St. Thomas says, that the pain of Purgatory exceeds anything that can be endured in this life: "The pain of Purgatory must exceed all pain of this life." And Dionysius the Carthusian relates that a dead person who had been raised to life by the intercession of St. Jerome, told St. Cyril of Jerusalem that all the torments of this earth are refreshing and delightful when compared with the very least pain of Purgatory: "If all the torments of the world were compared with the least that can be had in Purgatory they would appear comfortable" (*De Quat. Nov. a. 53*). And he adds that if a man had once tried those torments, he would rather suffer all the earthly sorrows that man can endure till the Day of Judgment, than suffer for one day the least pain of Purgatory. Hence St. Cyril wrote to St. Augustine: "That as far as regards the infliction of suffering, these pains are the same as those of Hell—their only difference being that they are not eternal" (*Int. Op. Aug. Ep. 19, E.B. app.*).

Hence we see that the pains of these holy souls are excessive, while, on the other hand, they cannot help themselves; because as Job says: "they are in chains, and are bound with the cords of poverty" (*Job 36: 8*). They are destined to reign with Christ, but they are withheld from taking possession of their kingdom till the time of their purgation is accomplished. And they cannot help themselves (at least not sufficiently, even according to those theologians who assert that they can by their prayers gain some relief) to throw off their chains, until they have entirely satisfied the justice of God. This is precisely what a Cistercian monk said to the sacristan of his monastery: "Help me, I beseech you, with your prayers; for of myself I can obtain nothing." And this is consistent with the saying of St. Bonaventure: "Destitution prevents solvency" (*Serm. de Mort.*). That is, those souls are so poor, that they have no means of making satisfaction.

On the other hand, since it is certain, and even of faith, that by our suffrages, and chiefly by our prayers, as particularly recommended and practiced by the Church, we can relieve those Holy Souls, I do not know how to excuse that man from sin who neglects to give them some assistance, at least by his prayers.

If a sense of duty will not persuade us to succour them, let us think of the pleasure it will give Jesus Christ to see us endeavouring to deliver his beloved spouses from prison, in order that he may have them with Him in Paradise. Let us think of the store of merit which we can lay up by practicing this great act of charity; let us think, too, that those souls are not ungrateful, and will never forget the great benefit we do them in relieving them of their pains, and in obtaining for them, by our prayers, anticipation of their entrance into glory; so that when they are there they will never neglect to pray for us. And if God promises mercy to him who practices mercy towards his neighbour—"Blessed are the merciful, for they shall obtain mercy" (*Matt. 5: 7*)—he may reasonably expect to be saved who remembers to assist those souls so afflicted, and yet so dear to God.

Jonathan, after having saved the Hebrews from ruin by a victory over their enemies, was condemned to death by his father Saul for having tasted some honey against his express commands; but the people came before the king, and said, "Shall Jonathan then die, who hath wrought this great salvation in Israel?" (*1 Sam. 14: 45*). So may we expect, that if any of us ever obtains, by his prayers, the liberation of a soul from Purgatory, that soul will say to God: "Lord, suffer not him who has delivered me from my torments to be lost."

And if Saul spared Jonathan's life at the request of his people, God will not refuse the salvation of a Christian to the prayers of a Soul which is his own spouse. Moreover, St. Augustine says that God will cause those who in this life have most succoured those Holy Souls, when they come to Purgatory themselves, to be most succoured by others. I may here observe that, in practice, one of the best suffrages is to hear Mass for them, and during the Holy Sacrifice to recommend them to God by the merits and Passion of Jesus Christ. The following form may be used: "Eternal Father, I offer Thee this Sacrifice of the Body and Blood of Jesus Christ, with all the pains which He suffered in His life and death; and by His Passion I recommend to Thee the souls in Purgatory, and especially that of," etc. And it is a very charitable act to recommend, at the same time, the souls of all those who are at the point of death.

4. Is it necessary to invoke the Saints?

Whatever doubt there may be whether or not the Souls in Purgatory can pray for us, and therefore whether or not it is of any use to recommend ourselves to their prayers, there can be no doubt whatever with regard to the Saints. For it is certain that it is most useful to have recourse to the intercession of the Saints canonised by the Church, who are already enjoying the vision of God.

To suppose that the Church can err in canonising is a sin or is heresy, according to St. Bonaventure, Bellarmine, and others; or at least next door to heresy, according to Suarez, Azorius, Gotti, etc.; because the Sovereign Pontiff, according to St. Thomas, is guided by the infallible influence of the Holy Ghost in an especial way when canonizing the Saints (*Quod. 9, a. 16, ad. 1*).

But to return to the question just proposed: are we obliged to have recourse to the intercession of the Saints? I do not wish to meddle with the decision of this question; but I cannot omit the exposition of a doctrine of St. Thomas. In several places above quoted, and especially in his book of Sentences, he expressly lays it down as certain that everyone is bound to pray, because (as he asserts) in no other way can the graces necessary for salvation be obtained from God, except by prayer: "Every man is bound to pray, from the fact that he is bound to procure spiritual good for himself, which can only be got from God; so it can only be obtained by asking it of God" (*In 4. Sent. d. 15, q. 4, a. 1*).

Then, in another place of the same book, he proposes the exact question, "Whether we are bound to pray to the Saints to intercede for us?" (*Dist. 45, q. 3, a. 2*). And he answers as follows—in order to catch his real meaning, we will quote the entire passage: "According to Dionysius, the order which God has instituted for his creature requires that things which are remote may be brought to God by means of things which are nearer to Him. Hence, as the Saints in Heaven are nearest of all to Him, the order of His law requires that we who 'remaining in the body are absent from the Lord,' should be brought to Him by means of the Saints; and this is effected by the Divine goodness pouring forth His gifts through them. And as the path of our return to God should correspond to the path of the good things which proceed from Him to us, it follows that, as the benefits of God come down to us by means of the suffrages of the Saints, we ought to be brought to God by the same way, so that a second time we may receive His benefits by the mediation of the Saints. Hence it is that we make them our intercessors with God, and as it were our mediators, when we ask them to pray for us."

Note well the words—"The order of God's law requires;" and especially note the last words—"As the benefits of God come down to us by means of the suffrages of the Saints, in the same way we must be brought back to God so that a second time we may receive His benefits by the mediation of the Saints."

So that, according to St. Thomas, the order of the Divine law requires that we mortals should be saved by means of the Saints, in that we receive by their intercession the help necessary for our salvation. He then puts the objection, that it appears superfluous to have recourse to the Saints, since God is infinitely more merciful than they, and more ready to hear us. This he answers by saying: "God has so ordered, not on account of any want of mercy on His part, but to keep the right order which He has universally established, of working by means of second causes. It is not for want of His mercy, but to preserve the aforesaid order in the creation."

In conformity with this doctrine of St. Thomas, the Continuator of Tourneley and Sylvius writes, that although God only is to be prayed to as the Author of grace, yet we are bound to have recourse also to the intercession of the Saints, so as to observe the order which God has established with regard to our salvation, which is, that the inferior should be saved by imploring the aid of the superior, "By the law of nature we are bound to observe the order which God has appointed; but God has appointed that the inferior should obtain salvation by imploring the assistance of his superior" (*De relig. p.2. c.2, a.5*).

4
The Intercession of the Blessed Virgin

And if this is true of the Saints, much more is it true of the intercession of the Mother of God, whose prayers are certainly of more value in His sight than those of all the rest of the Inhabitants of Heaven together.

For St. Thomas says that the Saints, in proportion to the merits by which they have obtained grace for themselves, are able also to save others; but that Jesus Christ, and so also his Mother, have merited so much grace that they can save all men. "It is a great thing in any Saint that he should have grace enough for the salvation of many beside himself; but if he had enough for the salvation of all men, this would be the greatest of all; and this is the case with Christ, and with the Blessed Virgin" (*Expos. in Sal. Aug.*).

And St. Bernard speaks thus to Mary: "Through thee we have access to thy Son, O discoverer of grace and Mother of salvation, that through thee He may receive us, who through thee was given to us" (*In Adv. Dom. s. 2*). These words signify that as we only have access to the Father by means of the Son, Who is the Mediator of justice, so we only have access to the Son by means of the Mother, who is mediator of grace, and who obtains for us, by her intercession, the gifts which Jesus Christ has merited for us.

And therefore St. Bernard says in another place that Mary has received a twofold fullness of grace. The first was the Incarnation of the Word, who was made Man in her most holy womb; the second is that fullness of grace which we receive from God by means of her prayers. Hence the Saint adds: "God has placed the fullness of all good in Mary, that if we have any hope, any grace, any salvation, we may know that it overflows from her who 'ascendeth abounding with delights" (*De Aquaed.*).

She is a garden of delights, whose doors spread abroad and abound; that is, the gifts of graces. So that whatever good we have from God, we receive all by the intercession of Mary. Why is this? Because, says St. Bernard, it is God's will: "Such is His will, who would have us receive everything through Mary."

But the more precise reason is deduced from the expression of St. Augustine, that Mary is justly called our Mother because she co-operated by her charity in the birth of the faithful to the life of grace, by which we become members of Jesus Christ, our head: "But clearly she is the mother of His members (which we are); because she cooperated by her charity in the birth of the faithful in the Church, and they are members of that Head" (*De S. Virginit. c. 6*). Therefore, as Mary co-operated by her charity in the spiritual birth of the faithful, so also God willed that she should co-operate by her intercession to make them enjoy the life of grace in this world and the life of glory in the next; and therefore the Church makes us call her and salute her without any circumlocution by the names, "our life, our sweetness, and our hope."

Hence St. Bernard exhorts us to have continual recourse to the Mother of God, because her prayers are certain to be heard by her Son: "Go to Mary, I say, without hesitation; the Son will hear the Mother." And then he says: "My children, she is the ladder of sinners, she is my chief confidence, she is the whole ground of my hope."

He calls her "ladder," because, as you cannot mount the third step except you first put your foot on the second, nor can you arrive at the second except by the first, so you cannot come to God except by means of Jesus Christ, nor can you come to Christ except by means of His Mother. Then he calls her "his greatest security, and the whole ground of his hope;" because, as he affirms, God wills that all the graces which He gives us should pass through the hands of Mary. And he concludes by saying that we ought to ask all the graces which we desire through Mary, because she obtains whatever she seeks, and her prayers cannot be rejected. "Let us seek grace, and let us seek it through Mary, because she obtains whatever she seeks; she finds, and she cannot be disappointed."

The following Saints teach the same as St. Bernard: St. Ephrem, "We have no other confidence than from thee, O purest Virgin!" St. Ildephonsus, "All the good things that the Divine Majesty has determined to give them, He has determined to commit to thy hands; for to thee are entrusted the treasures and the wardrobes of grace"(*De Cor. Virg. c. 15*). St. Germanus, "If thou desertest us, what will become of us, O life of Christians?" St. Peter Damian, "In thy hands are all the treasures of the mercies of God" (*De Nativ. s. 1*). St. Antonius, "Who seeks without her aid, attempts to fly without wings." St. Bernardine of Siena, "Thou art the dispenser of all graces; our salvation is in thy hands." In another place, he not only says that all graces are transmitted to us by means of Mary, but he also asserts that the Blessed Virgin, from the time she became Mother of God, acquired a certain jurisdiction over all the graces that are given to us. "Through the Virgin the vital graces are transfused from Christ, the Head, into His mystical body." "From the time when the Virgin Mother conceived in her womb the Word of God, she obtained a certain jurisdiction (if I may so speak) over every temporal procession of the Holy Ghost; so that no creature could obtain any grace from God, except by the dispensation of His sweet Mother." And he concludes, "Therefore all gifts, virtues, and graces are dispensed through her hands to whom she wills, and as she wills."

St. Bonaventure says the same: "Since the whole Divine nature was in the womb of the Virgin, I do not fear to teach that she has a certain jurisdiction over all the streams of grace, as her womb was, as it were, an ocean of the Divine nature, whence all the streams of grace must emanate."

On the authority of these Saints, many theologians have piously and reasonably defended the opinion that there is no grace given to us except by means of the intercession of Mary; so Mendoza, Vega, Paciucchelli, Segneri, Piore, Crasset, and others, as also the learned Alexander Natalis who says: "It is God's will that we should look to Him for all good things to be procured by the most powerful intercession of the Blessed Virgin, when we invoke her as it is fit" (*Ep. 50, in calce Theol.*). And he quotes in confirmation the passage of St. Bernard: "Such is His will who has determined that we should receive all through Mary."

Contenson says the same, in a comment on the words addressed by Jesus on the cross to St. John, "Behold thy Mother:" As though he had said, "No one shall be partaker of my blood except by the intercession of my Mother (*John 19: 27*). My wounds are fountains of grace, but their streams shall flow to on one, except through the canal of Mary. O my disciple John, I will love you as you love her!"

For the rest, it is certain, that if God is pleased when we have recourse to the Saints, He will be much more pleased when we avail ourselves of the intercession of Mary, that she, by her merits, may compensate for our unworthiness, according to the words of St. Anselm: "That the dignity of the intercessor may supply for our poverty. So that, to invoke the Virgin, is not to distrust God's mercy, but to fear our own unworthiness" (*De incarn. q. 37, a. 4, d. 23, s. 3*).

St. Thomas, speaking of her dignity, calls it, as it were, infinite: "From the fact that she is the Mother of God, she has a certain infinite dignity" (*P. 1, q. 25, a. 6, ad 4*). So that it may be said with reason that the prayers of Mary have more power with God than those of all Heaven together.

Conclusion of the Chapter

Let us conclude this first point by giving the gist of all that has been said hitherto. He who prays is certainly saved. He who prays not is certainly damned. All the blessed (except infants) have been saved by prayer. All the damned have been lost through not praying; if they had prayed, they would not have been lost. And this is, and will be, their greatest torment in Hell, to think how easily they might have been saved only by asking God for His grace, but that now it is too late—the time of prayer is over.

Chapter 2

The Power of Prayer

I
Excellence of Prayer and its Power with God

Our prayers are so dear to God, that He has appointed the Angels to present them to Him as soon as they come forth from our mouths. "The Angels," says St. Hilary, "preside over the prayers of the faithful, and offer them daily to God" (*In Matt. Can, 18*). This is that smoke of the incense, which are the prayers of Saints, which St. John saw ascending to God from the hands of the Angels (*Apoc. 8: 3*); and which he saw in another place represented by golden phials full of sweet odours, very acceptable to God.

But in order to understand better the value of prayers in God's sight, it is sufficient to read both in the Old and New Testaments the innumerable promises which God makes to the man that prays. "Cry to Me, and I will here thee" (*Ps. 49: 15*). "Call upon Me, and I will deliver thee" (*Jer. 33: 3*). "Ask, and it shall be given you; seek, and you shall find; knock, and it shall be opened unto you. He shall give good things to them that ask Him" (*Matt. 7: 7*). "Every one that asketh receiveth, and he that seeketh findeth" (*Luke 11: 10*). "Whatsoever they shall ask, it shall be done for them by My Father" (*John 15: 7*). "All things whatsoever you ask when you pray, believe that you shall receive them, and they shall come unto you" (*Matt. 18: 19*). "If you ask Me anything in My name, that will I do" (*Mark 11: 24*). "You shall ask whatever you will, and it shall be done unto you. Amen, amen, I say unto you, if you ask the Father anything in My name, He will give it to you" (*John 14: 14-16, 23*). There are a thousand similar texts; but it would take too long to quote them.

God wills us to be saved; but for our greater good, He wills us to be saved as conquerors. While, therefore, we remain here, we have to live in a continual warfare; and if we should be saved, we have to fight and conquer. "No one can be crowned without victory," says St. Chrysostom. We are very feeble, and our enemies are many and mighty; how shall we be able to stand against them, or to defeat them? Let us take courage, and say with the Apostle, "I can do all things in Him Who strengtheneth me" (*Phil. 4: 13*).

By prayer we can do all things for by this means God will give us that strength which we want. Theodoret says that prayer is omnipotent; it is but one, yet it can do all things: "Though prayer is one, it can do all things" And St. Bonaventure asserts that by prayer we obtain every good and escape every evil: "By it is obtained the gain of every good, and liberation from every evil." St. Laurence Justinian says that by means of prayer we build for ourselves a strong tower where we shall be secure from all the snares and assaults of our enemies: "By the exercise of prayer man is able to erect a citadel for himself." "The powers of Hell are mighty," says St. Bernard, "but prayer is stronger than all the devils."

Yes, for by prayer the soul obtains God's help which is stronger than any created power. Thus David encouraged himself in his alarms: "Praising I will call upon the Lord, and

I shall be saved from my enemies" (*Ps. 17: 4*). For, as St. Chrysostom says, "prayer is a strong weapon, a defence, a port, and a treasure" (*Hom. in Ps. 145*). It is a weapon sufficient to overcome every assault of the devil; it is a defence to preserve us in every danger; it is a port where we may be safe in every tempest; and it is at the same time a treasure which provides us with every good.

2
Power of Prayer against Temptation

God knows the great good which it does us to be obliged to pray, and therefore permits us (as we have already shown in the previous chapter) to be assaulted by our enemies, in order that we may ask Him for the help which He offers and promises to us. But as He is pleased when we run to Him in our dangers, so is He displeased when He sees us neglectful of prayer. "As the king," says St. Bonaventure, "would think it faithlessness in an officer, when his post was attacked, not to ask him for reinforcements, he would be reputed a traitor if he did not request help from the king;" so God thinks Himself betrayed by the man who, when he finds himself surrounded by temptations, does not run to Him for assistance. For He desires to help us and only waits to be asked, and then gives abundant succour.

This is strikingly shown by Isaias, when, on God's part, he told the king Achaz to ask some sign to assure himself of God's readiness to help him: "Ask thee a sign of the Lord Thy God" (*Is. 7: 2*). The faithless king answered: "I will not ask, and I will not tempt the Lord;" for he trusted in his own power to overcome his enemies without God's aid. And for this the Prophet reproved him: "Hear, therefore, O house of David; is it a small thing for you to be grievous to men, that you are grievous to my God also?" because that man is grievous and offensive to God who will not ask Him for the graces which He offers.

"Come to Me, all you that labour and are burdened, and I will refresh you" (*Matt. 11: 28*). "My poor children," says our Saviour, "though you find yourselves assailed by enemies, and oppressed with the weight of your sins, do not lose heart but have recourse to Me in prayer, and I will give you strength to resist, and I will give you a remedy for all your disasters." In another place he says, by the mouth of Isaias, "Come and accuse Me, saith the Lord; if your sins be as scarlet, they shall be made white as snow" (*Is. 1: 18*). O men, come to Me; though your consciences are horribly defiled, yet come; I even give you leave to reproach Me (so to speak), if after you had recourse to Me, I do not give you grace to become white as snow.

What is prayer? It is, as St. Chrysostom says, "the anchor of those tossed on the sea, the treasure of the poor, the cure of diseases, the safeguard of health." It is a secure anchor for him who is in peril of shipwreck; it is a treasury of immense wealth for him who is poor; it is a most efficacious medicine for him who is sick; and it is a certain preservative for him who would keep himself well.

What does prayer effect? Let us hear St. Laurence Justinian: "It pleases God, it gets what it asks, it overcomes enemies, it changes men." It appeases the wrath of God Who pardons all who pray with humility. It obtains every grace that is asked for; it vanquishes all the strength of the tempter, and it changes men from blind into seeing, from weak into strong, from sinners into Saints. Let him who wants light ask it of God, and it shall be given. As soon as I had recourse to God, says Solomon, He granted me wisdom: "I called upon God, and the Spirit of wisdom came to me" (*Wisd. 7: 7*). Let him who wants fortitude ask it of God, and it shall be given. As soon as I opened my mouth to pray, says David, I received help from God: "I opened my mouth, and drew in the Spirit" (*Ps. 118: 131*). And how in the world did the Martyrs obtain strength to resist tyrants, except by prayer, which gave them force to overcome dangers and death?

"He who uses this great weapon," says St. Chrysostom, "knows not death, leaves the earth, enters Heaven, lives with God." He falls not into sin; he loses affection for the earth; he makes his abode in Heaven; and begins, even in this life, to enjoy the conversation of God. How then can you disquiet such a man by saying: "How do you know that you are written in the book of life?" How do you know whether God will give you efficacious grace and the gift of perseverance? "Be nothing solicitous," says St. Paul, "but in everything by prayer and supplication, with thanksgiving, let your petitions be known unto God" (*Phil. 4: 6*). What is the use, says the Apostle, of agitating yourselves with these miseries and fears? Drive from you all these cares, which are of no use but to lessen your confidence, and to make you more tepid and slothful in walking along the way of salvation.

Pray and seek always, and make your prayers sound in God's ears, and thank Him for having promised to give you the gifts which you desire whenever you ask for them, namely efficacious grace, perseverance, salvation, and everything that you desire. The Lord has given us our post in the battle against powerful foes; but He is faithful in His promises, and will never allow us to be assaulted more violently than we can resist: "God is faithful, Who will not suffer you to be tempted above that which ye are able" (*1 Cor. 10: 13*).

He is faithful, since He instantly succours the man who invokes Him. The learned Cardinal Gatti writes that God has bound Himself not only to give us grace precisely balancing the temptation that assails us, but that He is obliged, when we are tempted and have recourse to Him, to afford us, by means of that grace which is kept ready for and offered to all, sufficient strength for us actually to resist the temptation. "God is bound, when we are tempted and fly to His protection, to give us by the grace prepared and offered to all such strength as will not only put us in the way of being able to resist, but will also make us resist; 'for we can do all things in Him who strengthens us' by His grace, if we humbly ask for it" (*De Grat., q. 2, d. 5, Sect. 3*).

We can do all things with God's help, which is granted to every one who humbly seeks it; so that we have no excuse when we allow ourselves to be overcome by a temptation. We are conquered solely by our own fault, because we would not pray. By prayer all the snares and power of the devil are easily overcome. "By prayer all hurtful things are chased away," says St. Augustine.

3
God is always ready to hear us

St. Bernardine of Siena says that prayer is a faithful ambassador, well known to the King of Heaven, and having access to His private chamber, and able by his importunity to induce the merciful heart of the King to grant every aid to us His wretched creatures, groaning in the midst of our conflicts and miseries in this valley of tears. "Prayer is a most faithful messenger, known to the King, who is used to enter His chamber, and by his importunity to influence the merciful mind of the King, and to obtain us assistance in our toils."

Isaias also assures us, that as soon as the Lord hears our prayers, He is moved with compassion towards us; and does not leave us to cry long to Him, but instantly replies, and grants us what we ask: "Weeping, thou shalt not weep, He will surely have pity upon thee: the voice of thy cry as soon as He shall hear, He will answer thee" (*Is. 30: 19*).

In another place He complains of us by the mouth of Jeremias: "Am I become a wilderness to Israel, or a lateward springing land? Why then have My people said, we are revolted, and will come to Thee no more?" (*Jer. 2: 31*) Why do you say that you will no more have recourse to Me? Has My mercy become to you a barren land which can yield you no fruits of grace? or a cold soil, which yields its fruit too late! So has our loving Lord assured us that He never neglects to hear us, and to hear us instantly when we pray; and so does He reproach those who neglect to pray through distrust of being heard.

If God were to allow us to present our petitions to Him once a month, even this would be a great favour. The kings of the earth give audiences a few times in the year, but God gives a continual audience. St. Chrysostom writes that God is always waiting to hear our prayers, and that a case never occurred when He neglected to hear a petition offered to Him properly: "God is always prepared for the voice of His servants, nor did He ever, when called upon as He ought to be, neglect to hear."

And in another place he says that when we pray to God, before we have finished recounting to Him our supplications, He has already heard us: "It is always obtained, even while we are yet praying." We even have the promise of God to do this: "As they are yet speaking, I will hear" (*Is. 45: 24*). The Lord, says

David, stands near to every one who prays, to console, to hear, and to save him: "The Lord is nigh to all them that call upon Him; to all that call upon Him in truth" (that is, as they ought to call). "He will do the will of them that fear Him; and He will hear their prayer and will save them" (*Ps. 146: 18*). This was it in which Moses gloried, when he said: "There is not another nation so great, that has gods so nigh them, as our God is present to all our petitions" (*Deut. 4: 7*). The gods of the Gentiles were deaf to those who invoked them, for they were wretched fabrications, which could do nothing. But our God, Who is Almighty, is not deaf to our prayers, but always stands near the man who prays, ready to grant him all the graces which he asks: "In what day soever I shall call upon Thee, behold I shall know that Thou art my God" (*Ps. 55: 10*). Lord, says the Psalmists, hereby do I know that Thou, my God, art all goodness and mercy, in that, whenever I have recourse to Thee, Thou dost instantly help me.

But to return to the question just proposed: are we obliged to have recourse to the intercession of the Saints? I do not wish to meddle with the decision of this question, but I cannot omit the exposition of a doctrine of St. Thomas.

In several places quoted above, and especially in his book of Sentences, he expressly lays it down as certain that everyone is bound to pray, because (as he asserts) in no other way can the graces necessary for salvation be obtained from God, except by prayer: "Every man is bound to pray from the fact that he is bound to procure spiritual good for himself which can only be got from God, so it can only be obtained by asking it of God" (*In 4. Sent. d. 15, q. 4, a. 1*).

Then, in another place of the same book, he proposes the exact question, "Whether we are bound to pray to the Saints to intercede for us?" (*Dist.45, q.3, a.2*) And he answers as follows—in order to catch his real meaning, we will quote the entire passage: "According to Dionysius, the order which God has instituted for His creature requires that things which are remote may be brought to God by means of things which are nearer to Him. Hence, as the Saints in Heaven are nearest of all to Him, the order of his law requires that we who 'remaining in the body are absent from the Lord,' should be brought to Him by means of the Saints; and this is effected by the Divine goodness pouring forth His gifts through them. And as the path of our return to God should correspond to the path of the good things which proceed from Him to us, it follows that, as the benefits of God come down to us by means of the suffrages of the Saints, we ought to be brought to God by the same way, so that a second time we may receive His benefits by the mediation of the Saints. Hence it is that we make them our intercessors with God, and as it were our mediators, when we ask them to pray for us."

Note well the words—"The order of God's law requires"; and especially note the last words—"As the benefits of God come down to us by means of the suffrages of the Saints, in the same way we must be brought back to God so that a second time we may receive his benefits by the mediation of the Saints." So that, according to St. Thomas, the order of the Divine law requires that we mortals should be saved by means of the Saints, in that we receive by their intercession the help necessary for our salvation.

He then puts the objection, that it appears superfluous to have recourse to the Saints, since God is infinitely more merciful than they, and more ready to hear us. This he answers by saying: "God has so ordered, not on account of any want of mercy on His part, but to keep the right order which He has universally established, of working by means of second causes. It is not for want of His mercy, but to preserve the aforesaid order in the creation."

In conformity with this doctrine of St. Thomas, the Continuator of Tourneley and Sylvius writes, that although God only is to be prayed to as the Author of grace, yet we are bound to have recourse also to the intercession of the Saints, so as to observe the order which God has established with regard to our salvation, which is, that the inferior should be saved by imploring the aid of the superior. "By the law of nature we are bound to observe the order which God has appointed; but God has appointed that the inferior should obtain salvation by imploring the assistance of his superior."

4
We should not limit ourselves to asking for little things; to pray is better than to meditate

We are so poor that we have nothing; but if we pray we are no longer poor. If we are poor, God is rich; and God, as the Apostle says, is all liberality to him that calls for His aid: "Rich unto all who call upon Him" (*Rom. 10: 12*). Since, therefore (as St. Augustine exhorts us), we have to do with a Lord of infinite power and infinite riches, let us not go to Him for little and valueless things, but let us ask some great thing of Him: "You seek from the Almighty,—seek something great" (*In. Ps. 62*).

If a man went to a king to ask some trumpery coin, like a farthing, me-thinks that man would but insult his king. On the other hand, we honour God, we honour His mercy, and His liberality, when, though we see how miserable we are, and how unworthy of any kindness, we yet ask for great graces, trusting in the goodness of God, and in His faithfulness to His promises of granting to the man who prays whatever grace he asks: "Whatsoever you will, ask, and it shall be done unto you" (*John 15: 7*).

St. Mary Magdalene of Pazzi said, "that God feels Himself so honoured and is so delighted when we ask for His grace, that He is, in a certain sense, grateful to us; because when we do this we seem to open to Him a way to do us a kindness, and to satisfy His nature, which is to do good to all." And let us be sure that, when we seek God's grace, He always gives us more than we ask: "If any of you want wisdom, let him ask of God, Who giveth to all abundantly, and upbraideth not" (*James 1: 5*). Thus speaks St. James, to show us that God is not like men, parsimonious of His goods; men though rich and liberal, when they give alms, are always somewhat close-handed, and generally give less than is asked of them, because their wealth, however great it be, is always finite, so that the more they give the less they have. But God, when He is asked, gives His good things "abundantly," and that is, with a generous hand, always giving more than is asked, because His wealth is infinite, and the more He gives the more He has to give: "For Thou, O Lord, art sweet and mild; and plenteous in mercy to all that call upon Thee" (*Ps. 85: 5*). Thou, O my God, said David, art but too liberal and kind to him that invokes Thee; the mercies which Thou pourest upon him are super-abundant, above all he asks.

On this point then we have to fix all our attention, namely, to pray with confidence, feeling sure that by prayer all the treasures of Heaven are thrown open to us. "Let us attend to this," says St. Chrysostom, "and we shall open Heaven to ourselves." Prayer is a treasure; he who prays most receives most.

St. Bonaventure says that every time a man has recourse to God by fervent prayer, he gains good things that are of more value than the whole world: "Any day a man gains more by devout prayer than the whole world is worth."

Some devout souls spend a great deal of time in reading and in meditating, but pay but little attention to prayer. There is no doubt that spiritual reading and meditation on the eternal truths are very useful things; "but," says St. Augustine, "it is of much more use to pray." By reading and meditating we learn our duty, but by prayer we obtain the grace to do it. "It is better to pray than to read: by reading we know what we ought to do; by prayer we receive what we ask." What is the use of knowing our duty, and then not doing it, but to make us more guilty in God's sight? Read and meditate as we like, we shall never satisfy our obligations, unless we ask of God the grace to fulfill them.

And, therefore, as St. Isidore observes, the devil is never more busy to distract us with the thoughts of worldly cares than when he perceives us praying and asking God for grace: "Then mostly does the devil insinuate thoughts, when he sees a man praying." And why? Because the enemy sees that at no other time do we gain so many treasures of Heavenly goods as when we pray.

This is the chief fruit of mental prayer, to ask God for the graces which we need for perseverance and for eternal salvation; and chiefly for this reason it is that mental prayer is morally necessary for the soul, to enable it to preserve itself in the grace of God. For if a person does not remember in the time of meditation to ask for the help necessary for perseverance, he will not do so at any other time; for without meditation he will not think of asking for it, and will not do so at any other time; for without meditation he will not think of asking for it, and will not even think of the necessity for asking it.

On the other hand, he who makes his meditation every day will easily see the needs of his soul, its dangers, and the necessity of his prayer; and so he will pray, and will obtain the graces which will enable him to persevere and save his soul. Father Segneri said of himself that when he began to meditate, he aimed rather at exciting affections than at making prayers. But when he came to know the necessity and the immense utility of prayer, he more and more applied himself, in his long mental prayer, to making petitions.

"As a young swallow, so will I cry," said the devout king Hezekias (*Is. 38: 14*). The young of the swallow does nothing but cry to its mother for help and for food; so should we all do, if we would preserve our life of grace. We should be always crying to God for aid to avoid the death of sin, and to advance in His holy love. Father Rodriguez relates that the ancient Fathers, who were our first instructors in the spiritual life, held a conference to determine which was the exercise most useful and most necessary for eternal salvation, and that they determined it was to repeat over and over again the short prayer of David, "Incline unto my aid, a God!" (*Ps. 69: 2*) "This," says Cassian, "is what every one ought to do who wishes to be saved: he ought to be always saying, My God, help me! my God, help me!"

We ought to do this the first thing when we awake in the morning; and then to continue doing it in all our needs, and when attending to our business, whether spiritual or temporal; and most especially when we find ourselves troubled by any temptation or passion. St. Bonaventure says that at times we obtain a grace by a short prayer sooner than by many other good works: "Sometimes a man can sooner obtain by a short prayer what he would be a long time obtaining by pious works." St. Ambrose says that he who prays, while he is praying obtains what he asks, because the very act of prayer is the same as receiving: "He who asks of God, while he asks receives; for to ask is to receive."

Hence St. Chrysostom wrote, that "there is nothing more powerful than a man who prays," because such a one is made partaker of the power of God. To arrive at perfection, says St. Bernard, we must meditate and pray: by meditation we see what we want; by prayer we receive what we want. "Let us mount by meditation and prayer: the one teaches what is deficient, and the other obtains that there should be nothing deficient."

Conclusion of the Chapter

In conclusion, to save one's soul without prayer is most difficult, and even (as we have seen). impossible, according to the ordinary course of God's Providence. But by praying our salvation is made secure, and very easy. It is not necessary in order to save our souls to go among the heathen and give up our life. It is not necessary to retire into the desert and eat nothing but herbs. What does it cost us to say, My God, help me! Lord, assist me! have mercy on me! Is there anything more easy than this? and this little will suffice to save us, if we will be diligent in doing it.

St. Laurence Justinian specially exhorts us to oblige ourselves to say a prayer at least when we begin any action: "We must endeavour to offer a prayer at least in the beginning of every work." Cassian attests that the principal advice of the ancient Fathers was to have recourse to God with short but frequent prayers. Let no one, says St. Bernard, think lightly of prayer, because God values it, and then gives us either what we ask, or what is still more useful to us: "Let no one undervalue his prayer, for God does not undervalue it… He will give either what we ask, or what He knows to be better" (*De Quad. S. 5*).

And let us understand that if we do not pray we have no excuse, because the grace of prayer is given to every one. It is in our power to pray whenever we will, as David says of himself: 'With me is prayer to the God of my life; I will say to God, Thou art my support" (*Ps. 41: 9*). On this point I shall speak at length in the second part, where I will make it quite clear that God gives to all the grace of prayer, in order that thereby they may obtain every help, and even more than they need, for keeping the Divine law and for persevering until death. At present I will only say, that if we are not saved, the whole fault will be ours and we shall have our own failure to answer for, because we did not pray.

Chapter 3

The Conditions of Prayer

I
Which are the requisite conditions

Object of Prayer

"Amen, amen, I say to you, if you ask the Father anything in My name, He will give it you" (*John 16: 23*). Jesus Christ then has promised that whatever we ask His Father in His name, His Father will give us, but always with the understanding that we ask under the proper conditions.

Many seek, says St. James, and obtain not because they seek improperly: "Ye ask and receive not, because ye ask amiss" (*James 4: 3*). So St. Basil, following out the argument of the Apostle, says, "You sometimes ask and receive not, because you have asked badly; either without faith, or you have requested things not fit for you, or you have not persevered;" "faithlessly," that is, with little faith, or little confidence; "lightly," with little desire of the grace you ask; "things not fit for you," when you seek good things that will not be conducive to your salvation; or you have left off praying, without perseverance.

Hence St. Thomas reduces to four the conditions required in prayer, in order that it may produce its effect: these are, that a man asks "(1) for himself; (2) things necessary for salvation; (3) piously; and (4) with perseverance" (*2. 2. q. 83, a. 15*).

Can we pray efficaciously for others?

The first condition then of prayer is that you make it "for yourself", because St. Thomas holds that one man cannot *ex condigno* (i.e. in the fitness of things) obtain for another eternal life; nor, consequently, even those graces which are requisite for his salvation. Since, as he says, the promise is made not to others, but only to those that pray: "He shall give to you."

Nevertheless, there are many theologians, Cornelius a Lapide, Sylvester, Tolet, Habert, and others, who hold the opposite doctrine, on the authority of St. Basil, who teaches that prayer, by virtue of God's promise, is infallibly efficacious, even for those for whom we pray, provided they put no positive impediment in the way. And they support their doctrine by Scripture: "Pray one for another, that you may be saved; for the continual prayer of the just man availeth much" (*James 5: 16*). "Pray for them that persecute and calumniate you" (*Luke 6: 28*).

And better still, on the text of St. John: "He that knoweth his brother to sin a sin which is not to death, let him ask, and life shall be given to him who sinneth and not unto death. There is a sin unto death; for that I say not that any man ask" (*1 John 5: 16*). St. Ambrose, St. Augustine, the Ven. Bede, and others, (*Apud. Calm. in loc. cit.*) explain the words "who sinneth not unto death," to mean, provided the sinner is not one who intends to remain obstinate till death; since for such a one a very extraordinary grace would be required. But for other sinners, who are not guilty of such malice, the Apostle promises their conversion to him who prays for them: "Let him ask, and life shall be given him for him that sinneth."

We ought to pray for sinners

Besides, it is quite certain that the prayers of others are of great use to sinners and are very pleasing to God, and God complains of His servants who do not recommend sinners to Him, as he once complained to St. Mary Magdalene of Pazzi, to whom He said one day: "See, my daughter, how the Christians are in the devil's hands; if my elect did not deliver them by their prayers they would be devoured."

But God especially requires this of priests and religious. The same Saint used to say to her nuns: "My sisters, God has not separated us from the world that we should only do good for ourselves, but also that we should appease Him in behalf of sinners;" and God one day said to her, "I have given to you my chosen spouses the City of Refuge (i.e., the Passion of Jesus Christ), that you may have a place where you may obtain help for My creatures. Therefore have recourse to it, and thence stretch forth a helping hand to My creatures who are perishing, and lay down your lives for them."

For this reason the Saint, inflamed with holy zeal, used to offer God the Blood of the Redeemer fifty times a day in behalf of sinners, and was quite wasted away for the desire she had for their conversion. Oh, she used to say, what pain is it, O Lord, to see how one could help Thy creatures by giving one's life for them, and not be able to do so! For the rest, in every exercise she recommended sinners to God; and it is written in her life, that she scarcely passed an hour in the day without praying for them. Frequently, too, she arose in the middle of the night and went to the Blessed Sacrament to pray for them; and yet for all this, when she was once found bathed in tears, on being asked the cause, she answered, "Because I seem to myself to do nothing for the salvation of sinners." She went so far as to offer to endure even the pains of Hell for their conversion, provided that in that place she might still love God; and often God gratified her by inflicting on her grievous pains and infirmities for the salvation of sinners. She prayed especially for priests, seeing that their good life was the occasion of salvation to others, while their bad life was the cause of ruin to many; and therefore she prayed God to visit their faults upon her, saying, "Lord, make me die and return to life again as many times as is necessary to satisfy Thy justice for them!" And it is related in her life that the Saint, by her prayers, did indeed release many souls from the hands of Lucifer.

I wished to speak rather particularly of the zeal of this Saint; but, indeed, no souls that really love God neglect to pray for poor sinners. For how it is possible for a person who loves God and knows what love He has for our souls and what Jesus Christ has done and suffered for their salvation and how our Saviour desires us to pray for sinners,—how is it possible, I say, that he should be able to look with indifference on the numbers of poor souls who are living without God, and are slaves of Hell, without being moved to importune God with frequent prayers to give light and strength to these wretched beings, so that they may come out from the miserable state of living death in which they are slumbering?

True it is that God has not promised to grant our requests when those for whom we pray put a positive impediment in the way of their conversion; but still, God of His goodness has often deigned, at the prayer of His servants, to bring back the most blinded and obstinate sinners to a state of salvation, by means of extraordinary graces.

Therefore, let us never omit, when we say or hear Mass, when we receive Holy Communion, when we make our meditation or our visit to the Blessed Sacrament, to recommend poor sinners to God. And a learned author says, that he who prays for others will find that his prayers for himself are heard much sooner. But this is a digression. Let us now return to the examination of the other conditions that St. Thomas lays down as necessary to the efficacy of prayer.

We must ask for the graces necessary to salvation

The second condition assigned by the Saint is that we ask those favours which are necessary to salvation, because the promise annexed to prayer was not made with reference to temporal favours which are not necessary for the salvation of the soul.

St. Augustine, explaining the words of the Gospel, "Whatever ye shall ask in My name," says that "nothing which is asked in a way detrimental to salvation is asked in the name of the Saviour" (*In Jo. tr. 102*). Sometimes, says the same Father, we seek some temporal favours, and God does not hear us, but He does not hear us because He loves us, and wishes to be merciful to us. "A man may pray faithfully for the necessities of this life, and God may mercifully refuse to hear him, because the physician knows better than the patient what is good for the sick man" (*Ap. s. Prosp. Sent. 212*).

The physician who loves his patient will not allow him to have those things that he sees would do him harm. Oh, how many, if they had been sick or poor, would have escaped those sins which they commit in health and in affluence! And, therefore, when men ask God for health or riches, He often denies them because He loves them, knowing that these things would be to them an occasion of losing His grace, or at any rate of growing tepid in the spiritual life. Not that we mean to say that it is any defect to pray to God for the necessaries of this present life, so far as they are not inconsistent with our eternal salvation, as the Wise man said: "Give me only the necessaries of life" (*Prov. 30: 8*). Nor is it a defect, says St. Thomas (*2. 2. q. 83, a. 6*), to have an anxiety about such goods, if it is not inordinate.

The defect consists in desiring and seeking these temporal goods, and in having an inordinate anxiety about them, as if they were our highest good. Therefore, when we ask of God these temporal favours, we ought always to ask them with resignation, and with the condition, if they will be useful to our souls; and when we see that God does not grant them, let us be certain that He then denies them to us for the love He bears us, and because He sees that they would be injurious to the salvation of our souls.

It often happens that we pray God to deliver us from some dangerous temptation, and yet that God does not hear us, but permits the temptation to continue troubling us. In such a case, let us understand that God permits even this for our greater good. It is not temptation or bad thoughts that separate us from God, but our consent to the evil.

When a soul in temptation recommends itself to God, and by His aid resists, oh, how it then advances in perfection, and unites itself more closely to God! and this is the reason why God does not hear it. St. Paul prayed instantly to be delivered from the temptation of impurity: "There was given me a sting of my flesh an angel of Satan to buffet me; for which thing thrice I besought the Lord, that it might depart from me" (*2 Cor. 12: 7*). But God answered him that it was enough to have His grace: "My grace is sufficient for thee" So that even in temptations we ought to pray with resignation, saying, "Lord, deliver me from this trouble if it is expedient to deliver me, and if not, at least give me help to resist."

And here comes in what St. Bernard says, that when we beg any grace of God, He gives us either that which we ask, or some other thing more useful to us. He often leaves us to be buffeted by the waves, in order to try our faithfulness, and for our greater profit. It seems then that He is deaf to our prayers. But no; let us be sure that God then really hears us, and secretly aids us, and strengthens us by His grace to resist all the assaults of our enemies. See how He Himself assures us of this by the mouth of the psalmist: "Thou calledst upon Me in affliction, and I delivered thee: I heard thee in the secret place of tempest; I proved thee at the waters of contradiction" (*Ps. 80: 8*).

Other conditions of prayer

The other conditions assigned by St. Thomas to prayer are, that it is to be made piously and perseveringly; by piously, he means with humility and confidence—by perseveringly, continuing to pray until death. We must now speak distinctly of each of these three conditions, which are the most necessary for prayer, namely of humility, confidence, and perseverance.

2
The humility with which we should pray

The Lord does indeed regard the prayers of His servants, but only of His servants who are humble. "He hath had regard to the prayer of the humble" (*Ps. 101: 18*). Others He does not regard, but rejects them: "God resisteth the proud, and giveth grace to the humble" (*James 4: 6*). He does not hear the prayers of the proud who trust in their own strength, but for that reason leaves them to their own feebleness, and in this state deprived of God's aid, they must certainly perish. David had to bewail this case: "Before I was humbled I offended" (*Ps. 118: 67*). I sinned because I was not humble.

The same thing happened to St. Peter, who, though he was warned by our Lord that all the disciples would abandon Him on that night—"All you shall be scandalized in Me this night" (*Matt. 26: 31*)—nevertheless, instead of acknowledging his own weakness and begging our Lord's aid against his unfaithfulness, was too confident in his own strength, and said that though all should abandon Him he would never leave Him: "Although all shall be scandalized in Thee, I will never be scandalized." And although our Saviour again foretold to him, in a special manner, that in that very night, before the cockcrow, he should deny Him three times, yet, trusting in his own courage, he boasted, saying, "Yea, though I should die with Thee, I will not deny Thee." But what came of it? Scarcely had the unhappy man entered the house of the high priest, when he was accused of being a disciple of Jesus Christ, and three times did he deny with an oath that he had ever known Him: "And again he denied with an oath, that I know not the Man." If Peter had humbled himself, and had asked our Lord for the grace of constancy, he would not have denied Him.

We ought all to feel that we are standing on the edge of a precipice, suspended over the abyss of all sins, and supported only by the thread of God's grace. If this thread fails us, we shall certainly fall into the gulf, and shall commit the most horrible wickedness. "Unless the Lord had been my helper, my soul had almost dwelt in Hell" (*Ps. 93: 17*). If God had not succoured me, I should have fallen into a thousand sins, and now I should be in Hell. So said the Psalmist, and so ought each of us to say. This is what St. Francis of Assisi meant when he said that he was the worst sinner in the world. "But, my Father," said his companion, "what you say is not true; there are many in the world who are certainly worse than you are." "Yes, what I say is but too true," answered St. Francis, "because if God did not keep His hand over me, I should commit every possible sin."

It is of faith that without the aid of grace we cannot do any good work, nor even think a good thought. "Without grace men do no good whatever, either in thought or in deed," says St. Augustine (*De Corr. et Gr. c. 2*). As the eye cannot see without light, so, says the holy Father, man can do not good without grace. The Apostle had said the same thing before him: "Not that we are sufficient to think anything of ourselves, as of ourselves; but our sufficiency is of God" (*2 Cor. 3: 5*). And David had said it before St. Paul: "Unless the Lord build the house, they labour in vain that build it" (*Ps. 126: 1*).

In vain does man weary himself to become a Saint, unless God lends a helping hand: "Unless the Lord keep the city, he watcheth in vain that keepeth it." If God did not preserve the soul from sins, in vain will it try to preserve itself by its own strength: and therefore did the holy prophet protest, "I will not trust in my bow" (*Ps. 43: 7*). I will not hope in my arms, but only in God, Who alone can save me.

Hence, whoever finds that he has done any good, and does not find that he has fallen into greater sins than those which are commonly committed, let him say with St. Paul, "By the grace of God I am what I am" (*1 Cor. 15: 10*), and for the same reason he ought never to cease to be afraid of falling on every occasion of sin: "Wherefore, he that thinketh himself to stand, let him take heed lest he fall" (*1 Cor. 10: 12*). St. Paul wishes to warn us that he who feels secure of not falling, is in great danger of falling; and he assigns the reason in another place, where he says, "If any man think himself to be something, whereas he is nothing, he deceiveth himself" (*Gal. 6: 3*).

So that St. Augustine wrote wisely, "the presumption of stability renders many unstable; no one will be so firm as he who feels himself infirm" (*Serm. 76 E.B.*). If a man says he has no fear, it is a sign that he trusts in himself, and in his good resolutions; but such a man, with his mischievous confidence, deceives himself, because, through trust in his own strength, he neglects to fear; and through not fearing he neglects to recommend himself to God, and then he will certainly fall.

And so, for like reasons, we should all abstain from noticing with any vainglory the sins of other people, but rather we should then esteem ourselves as worse in ourselves than they are, and should say, "Lord, if Thou hadst not helped, I should have done worse." Otherwise, to punish us for our pride, God will permit us to fall into worse and more shameful sins.

For this cause St. Paul instructs us to labour for our salvation; but how? Always in fear and trembling: "With fear and trembling work out your salvation" (*Phil. 2: 12*). Yes, for he who has a great fear of falling distrusts his own strength, and therefore places his confidence in God and will have recourse to Him in dangers; and God will aid him, and so he will vanquish his temptations and will be saved. St. Philip Neri, walking one day through Rome, kept saying, "I am in despair!" A certain religious rebuked him, and the Saint thereupon said, "My father, I am in despair for myself; but I trust in God."

So must we do, if we would be saved; we must always live in despair of doing anything by our own strength; and in so doing we shall imitate St. Philip who used to say to God the first moment he woke in the morning, "Lord, keep Thy hands over Philip this day; for if not, Philip will betray Thee."

This, then, we may conclude with St. Augustine, is all the grand science of a Christian,—to know that he is nothing, and can do nothing. "This is the whole of the great science, to know that man is nothing" (*In Ps. 70, S. 1*). For then he will never neglect to furnish himself, by prayer to God, with that strength which he has not of himself, and which he needs in order to resist temptation and to do good; and so, with the help of God, Who never refuses anything to the man who prays to Him in humility, he will be able to do all things: "The prayer of him that humbleth himself shall pierce the clouds, and he will not depart until the Most High behold" (*Ecclus. 35: 21*).

The prayer of a humble soul penetrates the heavens, and presents itself before the throne of God, and departs not without God's looking on it and hearing it. And though the soul be guilty of any amount of sin, God never despises a heart that humbles itself: "A contrite and humble heart, O God, Thou wilt not despise" (*Ps. 1: 19*); "God resisteth the proud, but giveth grace to the humble" (*James 4: 6*). As the Lord is severe with the proud, and resists their prayers, so is He kind and liberal to the humble. This is precisely what Jesus Christ said one day to St. Catherine of Siena: "Know, my daughter, that a soul that perseveres in humble prayer gains every virtue."

It will be of use to introduce here the advice which the learned and pious Palafox, Bishop of Osma, gives to spiritual persons who desire to become Saints. It occurs in a note to the 18th letter of St. Teresa, which she wrote to her Confessor, to give him an account of all the grades of supernatural prayer with which God had favoured her. On this the bishop writes that these supernatural graces which God designed to grant to St. Teresa, as He has also done to other Saints, are not necessary in order to arrive at sanctity, since many souls have become Saints without them; and, on the other hand, many have arrived at sanctity, and yet have, after all, been damned. Therefore he says it is superfluous, and even presumptuous, to desire and to ask for these supernatural gifts, when the true and only way to become a Saint is to exercise ourselves in virtue and in the love of God; and this is done by means of prayer, and by corresponding to the inspirations and assistance of God Who wishes nothing so much as to see us Saints. "For this is the will of God, your sanctification" (*1 Thess. 4: 3*).

Hence Bishop Palafox, speaking of the grades of supernatural prayer mentioned in St. Teresa's letter, namely, the prayer of quiet, the sleep or suspension of the faculties, the prayer of union, ecstasy or rapture, flight and impulse of the spirit, and the wound of love, says, very wisely, that as regards the prayer of quiet, what we ought to ask of God is that He would free us from attachment to worldly goods and the desire of them, which give no peace but bring disquiet and affliction to the soul: "Vanity of vanities," as Solomon well called them, "and vexation of spirit" (*Eccles. 1: 14*). The heart of man will never find true peace if it does not empty itself of all that is not God so as to leave itself all free for His love, that He alone may possess the whole of it. But this the soul cannot do of itself; it must obtain it of God by repeated prayers.

As regards "the sleep and suspension of the faculties", we ought to ask God for grace to keep them asleep for all that is temporal, and only awake them to consider God's goodness and to set our hearts upon His love and eternal happiness.

As regards the "union of the faculties", let us pray Him to give us grace not to think, nor to seek, nor to wish anything but what God wills, since all sanctity and the perfection of love consists in uniting our will to the will of God.

As regards "ecstasy and rapture", let us pray God to draw us away from the inordinate love of ourselves and of creatures, and to draw us entirely to Himself.

As regards "the flight of the spirit", let us pray Him to give us grace to live altogether detached from this world, and to do as the swallows that do not settle on the ground even to feed, but take their food flying;—so should we use our temporal goods for all that is necessary for the support of life, but always flying, without settling on the ground to look for earthly pleasures.

As regards "impulse of spirit", let us pray Him to give us courage and strength to do violence to ourselves, whenever it is necessary, for resisting the assaults of our enemies, for conquering our passions, and for accepting sufferings even in the midst of desolation and dryness of spirit.

Finally, as regards "the wound of love", as a wound by its pain perpetually renews the remembrance of what we suffer, so ought we to pray God to wound our hearts with His holy love in such a way that we shall always be reminded of His goodness and the love which He has borne us, and thus we should live in continual love of Him and should be always pleasing Him with our works and our affections. But none of these graces can be obtained without prayer, and with prayer, provided it be humble, confident, and persevering, everything is obtained.

3
The confidence with which we should pray

Excellence and necessity of this virtue

The principal instruction that St. James gives us, if we wish by prayer to obtain grace from God, is that we pray with a confidence that feels sure of being heard, and without hesitating: "Let him ask in faith, nothing wavering" (*James 1: 6*).

St. Thomas teaches that as prayer receives its power of meriting from charity, so, on the other hand, it receives from faith and confidence its power of being efficacious to obtain: "Prayer has its power of meriting from charity, but its efficacy of obtaining from faith and confidence" (*2. 2. q. 83, a. 15*). St. Bernard teaches the same, saying that it is our confidence alone which obtains for us the Divine mercies: "Hope alone obtains a place of mercy with Thee, O Lord."

God is much pleased with our confidence in His mercy, because we then honour and exalt that infinite goodness which it was His object in creating us to manifest to the world: "Let all those, O my God", says the royal prophet, who hope in Thee be glad, for they shall be eternally happy, and Thou shalt dwell in them" (*Ps. 5: 12*). God protects and saves all those who confide in Him: "He is the Protector of all that hope in Him" (*Ps. 17: 31*). "Thou who savest them that trust in Thee" (*Ps. 16: 7*).

Oh, the great promises that are recorded in the Scriptures to all those who hope in God! He who hopes in God will not fall into sin: "None of them that trust in Him shall offend" (*Ps. 33: 23*). Yes, says David, because God has His eyes turned to all those who confide in His goodness to deliver them by His aid from the death of sin. "Behold, they eyes of the Lord are on them that fear Him, and on them that hope for His mercy to deliver their souls from death" (*Ps. 32: 18*). And in another place God Himself says: "Because he hoped in Me I will deliver him; I will protect him; I will deliver him and I will glorify him" (*Ps. 90: 14*). Mark the word "because." "Because" he confided in Me, I will protect, I will deliver him from his enemies, and from the danger of falling; and finally I will give him eternal glory.

Isaias says of those who place their hope in God: "They that hope in the Lord shall renew their strength; they shall take wings as the eagles; they shall run and not be weary: they shall walk and not faint" (*Is. 40: 31*). They shall cease to be weak as they are now and shall gain in God a great strength; they shall not faint; they shall not even feel weary in walking the way of salvation, but they shall run and fly as eagles; "in silence and in hope shall your strength be" (*Is. 30: 15*). All our strength, the prophet tells us, consists in placing all our confidence in God and in being silent; that is, in reposing in the arms of His mercy, without trusting to our own efforts, or to human means.

And when did it ever happen that a man had confidence in God and was lost? "No one hath hoped in the Lord and hath been confounded" (*Ecclus. 2: 11*).

It was this confidence that assured David that he should not perish: "In Thee, O Lord, have I trusted; I shall not be confounded forever" (*Ps. 30: 2*). Perhaps, then, says St. Augustine, God could be a deceiver Who offers to support us in dangers if we lean upon Him, and would then withdraw Himself if we had recourse to Him? "God is not a deceiver that He should offer to support us and then when we lean upon Him should slip away from us." David calls the man happy who trusts in God: "Blessed is the man that trusteth in Thee" (*Ps. 83: 13*). And why? Because, says he, he who trusts in God will always find himself surrounded by God's mercy. "Mercy shall encompass him that hopeth in the Lord" (*Ps. 31: 10*). So that he shall be surrounded and guarded by God on every side in such a way that he shall be prevented from losing his soul.

It is for this cause that the Apostle recommends us so earnestly to preserve our confidence in God; for (he tells us). it will certainly obtain from him a great remuneration: "Do not therefore lose your confidence, which hath a great reward" (*Heb. 10: 35*). As in our confidence, so shall be the graces we receive from God: if our confidence is great, great too will be the graces: "Great faith merits great things."

St. Bernard writes that the Divine mercy is an inexhaustible fountain, and that he who brings to it the largest vessel of confidence shall take from it the largest measure of gifts: "Neither, O Lord, dost Thou put the oil of Thy mercy into any other vessel than that of confidence." The Prophet had long before expressed the same thought: "Let Thy mercy, O Lord, be upon us as (i.e., in proportion) we have hoped in Thee" (*Ps. 32: 22*). This was well exemplified in the centurion to whom our Saviour said, in praise of his confidence, "Go, and as thou hast believed, so be it done unto thee" (*Matt. 8: 12*). And our Lord revealed to St. Gertrude that he who prays with confidence does Him in a manner such violence that He cannot but hear him in everything he asks: "Prayer," says St. John Climacus, "does a pious violence to God." It does Him a violence, but a violence which He likes, and which pleases Him.

"Let us go, therefore," according to the admonition of St. Paul, "with confidence to the throne of grace, that we may obtain mercy, and find grace in seasonable aid" (*Heb. 4: 16*). The throne of grace is Jesus Christ, Who is now sitting on the right hand of the Father; not on the throne of justice, but of grace, to obtain pardon for us if we fall into sin, and help to enable us to persevere if we are enjoying His friendship.

To this throne we must always have recourse with confidence; that is to say, with that trust which springs from faith in the goodness and truth of God, Who has promised to hear him who prays to Him with confidence, but with a confidence that is both sure and stable.

On the other hand, says St. James, let not the man who prays with hesitation think that he will receive anything: "For he who wavereth is like a wave of the sea, which is moved and carried about by the wind. Therefore let not that man think to receive anything of the Lord" (*James 1: 6*). He will receive nothing, because the diffidence which agitates him is unjust towards God, and will hinder His mercy from listening to his prayers: "Thou hast not asked rightly, because thou hast asked doubtingly," says St. Basil; "thou hast not received grace, because thou hast asked it without confidence."

David says that our confidence in God ought to be as firm as a mountain, which is not moved by each gust of wind. "They who trust in the Lord are as Mount Sion; He shall not be moved forever" (*Ps. 124: 1*). And it is this that our Lord recommends to us if we wish to obtain the graces which we ask: "Whatsoever you ask when you pray, believe that you shall receive, and they shall come unto you" (*Mark 11: 24*). Whatever grace you require, be sure of having it, and so you shall obtain it.

Foundation of our confidence

But on what, a man will say, am I, a miserable sinner, to found this certain confidence of obtaining what I ask? On what? On the promise made by Jesus Christ: "Ask, and you shall receive" (*John 16: 24*). "Who will fear to be deceived, when the truth promises?" says St. Augustine. How can we doubt that we shall be heard, when God, Who is truth itself, promises to give us that which we ask of Him in prayer? "We should not be exhorted to ask," says the same Father, "unless He meant to give."

Certainly God would not have exhorted us to ask Him for favours, if He had not determined to grant them; but this is the very thing to which He exhorts us so strongly, and which is repeated so often in the Scriptures—pray, ask, seek, and you shall obtain what you desire: "Whatever you will, seek and it shall be done to you" (*John 15: 7*). And in order that we may pray to Him with due confidence, our Saviour has taught us in the "Our Father" that when we have recourse to Him for the graces necessary to salvation (all of which are included in the petitions of the Lord's Prayer) we should call Him, not Lord, but Father—"Our Father"—because it is His will that we should ask God for grace with the same confidence with which a son, when in want or sick, asks food or medicine from his own father.

If a son is dying of hunger, he has only to make his case known to his father, and his father will forthwith provide him with food; and if he has received a bite from a venomous serpent, he has only to show his father the wound, and the father will immediately apply whatever remedy he has.

Trusting, therefore, in God's promises, let us always pray with confidence; not vacillating, but stable and firm, as the Apostle says: "Let us hold fast the confession of our hope without wavering; for He is faithful that hath promised" (*Heb. 10: 23*). As it is perfectly certain that God is faithful in His promises, so ought our faith also to be perfectly certain that He will hear us when we pray. And although sometimes, when we are in a state of aridity, or disturbed by some fault we have committed, we perhaps do not feel while praying that sensible confidence which we would wish to experience, yet, for all this, let us force ourselves to pray, and to pray without ceasing; for God will not neglect to hear us. Nay, rather He will hear us more readily, because we shall then pray with more distrust of ourselves and confiding only in the goodness and faithfulness of God, Who has promised to hear the man who prays to Him. Oh, how God is pleased in the time of our tribulations, of our fears, and of our temptations, to see us hope against hope; that is, in spite of the feeling of diffidence which we then experience because of our desolation! This is that for which the Apostle praises the patriarch Abraham, "who against hope, believed in hope" (*Rom. 4: 18*).

St. John says that he who reposes a sure trust in God certainly will become a Saint: "And every one that hath this hope in Him sanctifieth himself, as he also is holy" (*1 John 3: 3*). For God gives abundant graces to them that trust in Him. By this confidence the host of Martyrs, of Virgins, even of children, in spite of the dread of the torments which their persecutors prepared for them, overcame both their tortures and their persecutors. Sometimes, I say, we pray, but it seems to us that God will not hear us. Alas!

Let us not then neglect to persevere in prayer and in hope; let us then say, with Job, "Although He should kill me, I will trust in Him" (*Job 13: 15*). O my God! Though Thou hast driven me from Thy presence, I will not cease to pray and to hope in Thy mercy. Let us do so, and we shall obtain what we want from God. So did the Canaanite woman, and she obtained all that she wished from Jesus Christ. This woman had a daughter possessed by a devil, and prayed our Saviour to deliver her: "Have mercy on me, my daughter is grievously tormented by a devil" (*Matt. 15: 22*). Our Lord answered her that He was not sent for the Gentiles, of whom she was one, but for the Jews. She, however, did not lose heart, but renewed her prayer with confidence: Lord, Thou canst console me! Thou must console me: "Lord, help me!" Jesus answered, but as to the bread of the children, it is not good to give it to the dogs: "It is not good to take the children's bread and to cast it to the dogs." But, my Lord, she answered, even the dogs are allowed to have the fragments of bread which fall from the table: "Yea, Lord; for the whelps eat of the crumbs that fall from the tables of their masters."

Then our Saviour, seeing the great confidence of this woman, praised her, and did what she asked, saying: "O woman, great is thy faith; be it done to thee as thou wilt." For who, says Ecclesiasticus, has ever called on God for aid, and has been neglected and left unaided by Him? "Or who hath called upon Him, and He hath despised him?" (*Ecclus. 2: 12*)

St. Augustine says that prayer is a key which opens Heaven to us; the same moment in which our prayer ascends to God, the grace which we ask for descends to us: "The prayer of the just is the key of Heaven; the petition ascends, and the mercy of God descends" (*Serm. 47. E.B. app.*). The royal prophet writes that our supplications and God's mercy are united together: "Blessed is God, Who has not turned away my prayer nor His mercy for me" (*Ps. 65: 20*). And hence the same St. Augustine says that when we are praying to God, we ought to be certain that God is hearing us: "When you see that your prayer is not removed from you, be sure that His mercy is not removed from you" (*In Ps. 65*).

And for myself, I speak the truth, I never feel greater consolation nor a greater confidence of my salvation than when I am praying to God and recommending myself to Him. And I think that the same thing happens to all other believers, for the other signs of our salvation are uncertain and unstable, but that God hears the man who prays to Him with confidence is an infallible truth, as it is infallible that God cannot fail in His promises.

When we find ourselves weak and unable to overcome any passion or any great difficulty so as to fulfill that which God requires of us, let us take courage and say, with the Apostle, "I can do all things in Him Who strengtheneth me" (*Phil. 4: 13*).

Let us not say, as some do: I cannot; I distrust myself. With our own strength certainly we can do nothing, but with God's help we can do everything. If God said to anyone, take this mountain on your back and carry it, for I am helping you, would not the man be a mistrustful fool if he answered: I will not take it, for I have not strength to carry it? And thus, when we know how miserable and weak we are, and when we find ourselves most encompassed with temptations, let us not lose heart, but let us lift up our eyes to God and say with David, "The Lord is my helper; and I will despise my enemies" (*Ps. 117: 7*).

With the help of my Lord, I shall overcome and laugh to scorn all the assaults of my foes. And when we find ourselves in danger of offending God or in any other critical position and are too confused to know what is best to be done, let us recommend ourselves to God, saying, "The Lord is my light and my salvation; whom shall I fear?" (*Ps. 26: 1*) And let us be sure that God will then certainly give us light and will save us from every evil.

The prayer of sinners

But I am a sinner, you will say, and in the Scriptures I read, "God heareth not sinners" (*John 9: 31*). St. Thomas answers (with St. Augustine) that this was said by the blind man who, when he spoke, had not as yet been enlightened: "That is the word of a blind man not yet perfectly enlightened, and therefore it is not authoritative" (*2. 2. q. 83, a. 16*). Though, adds St. Thomas, it is true of the petition which the sinner makes, "so far forth as he is a sinner;" that is, when he asks from a desire of continuing to sin; as, for instance, if he were to ask assistance to enable him to take revenge on his enemy, or to execute any other bad intention. The same holds good for the sinner who prays God to save him, but has no desire to quit the state of sin.

There are some unhappy persons who love the chains with which the devil keeps them bound like slaves. The prayers of such men are not heard by God, because they are rash, presumptuous and abominable. For what greater presumption can there be than for a man to ask favours of a prince whom he not only has often offended, but whom he intends to offend still more? And this is the meaning of the Holy Spirit, when he says that the prayer of him who turns away his ears so as not to hear what God commands is detestable and odious to God: "He who turneth away his ears from learning the law, his prayer shall be an abomination" (*Prov. 28: 9*).

To these people God says: it is of no use your praying to Me for I will turn My eyes from you and will not hear you: "When you stretch forth your hands, I will turn away My eyes from you; and when you multiply prayer, I will not hear" (*Is. 1: 15*). Such, precisely, was the prayer of the impious King Antiochus, who prayed to God and made great promises, but insincerely, and with a heart obstinate in sin; the sole object of his prayer being to escape the punishment that impended over him. Therefore God did not hear his prayer, but caused him to die devoured by worms: "Then this wicked man prayed to the Lord, of Whom he was not to obtain mercy" (*1 Mach. 1: 13*).

But others, who sin through frailty or by the violence of some great passion, and who groan under the yoke of the enemy, and desire to break these chains of death and to escape from their miserable slavery, and therefore ask the assistance of God, the prayer of these, if it is persevering, will certainly be heard by Him Who says that every one that asks receives, and he who seeks grace finds it: "For every one that asketh receiveth, and he that seeketh findeth" (*Matt. 7: 8*). "Every one, whether he be a just man or a sinner," says the author of the *Opus Imperfectum*.

And in St. Luke, our Lord, when speaking of the man who gave all the loaves he had to his friend, not so much on account of his friendship as because of the other's importunity, says, "If he shall continue knocking, I say to you, although he will not rise and give him because he is his friend, yet because of his importunity he will rise and give him as many as he needeth" (*Luke 11: 8*). "And so I say unto you: Ask, and it shall be given to you." So that persevering prayer obtains mercy from God, even for those who are not His friends.

That which is not obtained through friendship, says St. Chrysostom, is obtained by prayer: "That which was not effected by friendship was effected by prayer." He even says that prayer is valued more by God than friendship: "Friendship is not of such avail with God as prayer; that which is not effected by friendship is effected by prayer." And St. Basil doubts not that even sinners obtain what they ask if they persevere in praying: "Sinners obtain what they seek, if they seek perseveringly." St. Gregory says the same: "The sinner also shall cry, and his prayer shall reach to God." So St. Jerome, who says that even the sinner can call God his Father, if he prays to Him to receive him anew as a son; after the example of the Prodigal Son, who called Him Father, "Father, I have sinned," (*Luke 15: 21*) even though he had not as yet been pardoned.

If God did not hear sinners, says St. Augustine, in vain would the Publican have asked for forgiveness: "If God does not hear sinners, in vain would that Publican have said, God be merciful to me a sinner." But the Gospel assures us that the Publican did by his prayer obtain forgiveness: "This man went down to his house justified" (*Luke 18: 14*).

But further still, St. Thomas examines this point more minutely, and does not hesitate to affirm that even the sinner is heard if he prays; for though his prayer is not meritorious, yet it has the power of impetration,—that is, of obtaining what we ask, because impetration is not founded on God's justice, but on His goodness. "Merit," he says, "depends on justice; impetration, on grace" (*2. 2. q. 83, a. 16*). Thus did Daniel pray, "Incline, O my God, thine ear and hear... For not in our justifications do we present our prayers before Thy face, but in the multitude of Thy mercies" (*Dan. 9: 18*). Therefore, when we pray, says St. Thomas, it is not necessary to be friends of God, in order to obtain the grace we ask; for prayer itself renders us His friends: "Prayer itself makes us of the family of God."

Moreover, St. Bernard uses a beautiful explanation of this, saying that the prayer of a sinner to escape from sin arises from the desire to return to the grace of God. Now this desire is a gift, which is certainly given by no other than God Himself; to what end, therefore, says St. Bernard, would God give to a sinner this holy desire, unless He meant to hear him? "For what would He give the desire, unless He willed to hear?" And, indeed, in the Holy Scriptures themselves there are multitudes of instances of sinners who have been delivered from sin by prayer. Thus was King Achab delivered (*3 Kings 21: 27*), thus King Manasses (*2 Par. 33: 12*), thus King Nabuchodonosor (*Dan. 4: 31*) and thus the good thief (*Luke 23: 42*). Oh, the wonderful! oh, the mighty power of prayer! Two sinners are dying on Calvary by the side of Jesus Christ: one, because he prays, "Remember me," is saved; the other, because he prays not, is damned.

And, in fine, St. Chrysostom says, "No man has with sorrow asked favours from Him, without obtaining what he wished." No sinner has ever with penitence prayed to God, without having his desires granted. But why should we cite more authorities and give more reasons to demonstrate this point, when Our Lord Himself says, "Come to me, all you that labour and are burdened, and I will refresh you" (*Matt. 11: 28*). The "burdened," according to Saints Augustine, Jerome, and others, are sinners in general, who groan under the load of their sins, and who, if they have recourse to God, will surely, according to His promise, be refreshed and saved by His grace.

Ah, we cannot desire to be pardoned as much as He longs to pardon us. "Thou dost not," says St. Chrysostom, "so much desire thy sins to be forgiven, as He desires to forgive thy sins." There is no grace, he goes on to say, that is not obtained by prayer, though it be the prayer of the most abandoned sinner, provided only it be persevering: "There is nothing which prayer cannot obtain, though a man be guilty of a thousand sins, provided it be fervent and unremitting." And let us mark well the words of St. James: "If any man wanteth wisdom, let him ask of God, Who giveth to all abundantly, and upbraideth not" (*James 1: 5*). All those, therefore, who pray to God, are infallibly heard by Him and receive grace in abundance: "He giveth to all abundantly." But you should particularly remark the words which follow, "and upbraideth not." This means that God does not do as men, who, when a person who has formerly done them an injury comes to ask a favour, immediately upbraid him with his offence. God does not do so to the man who prays, even though he were the greatest sinner in the world, when he asks for some grace conducive to his eternal salvation. Then He does not upbraid him with the offences he has committed; but, as though he had never displeased Him, He instantly receives him, He consoles him, He hears him, and enriches him with an abundance of His gifts.

To crown all, our Saviour, in order to encourage us to pray, says "Amen, amen, I say to you, if you ask the Father anything in My name, He will give it you" (*John 16: 23*). As though He had said, Courage, O sinners, do not despair: do not let your sins turn away from having recourse to My Father, and from hoping to be saved by Him, if you desire it. You have not now any merits to obtain the graces which you ask for, for you only deserve to be punished; still do this: go to My Father in My name, through My merits ask the favours which you want, and I promise and swear to you ("Amen, amen, I say to you," which, according to St. Augustine, is a species of oath) that whatever you ask, My Father will grant. O God, what greater comfort can a sinner have after his fall than to know for certain that all he asks from God in the name of Jesus Christ will be given to him!

I say "all" but I mean only that which has reference to his eternal salvation; for with respect to temporal goods, we have already shown that God even when asked, sometimes does not give them, because He sees that they would injure our soul. But so far as relates to spiritual goods, His promise to hear us is not conditional, but absolute; and therefore St. Augustine tells us, that those things which God promises absolutely, we should demand with absolute certainty of receiving: "Those things which God promises, seek with certainty" (*Serm 354, E.B.*). And how much more does God desire to dispense His graces to us, says the Saint, than we to receive them! "He is more willing to be munificent of His benefits to thee than thou art desirous to receive them" (*Serm 105, E.B.*).

St. Chrysostom says that the only time when God is angry with us is when we neglect to ask Him for his gifts: "He is only angry when we do not pray." And how can it ever happen that God will not hear a soul who asks Him for favours all according to His pleasure? When the soul says to Him: Lord, I ask Thee not for goods of this world,—riches, pleasures, honours; I ask Thee only for Thy grace: deliver me from sin, grant me a good death, give me Paradise, give me Thy holy love (which is that grace which St. Francis de Sales says we should seek more than all others), give me resignation to Thy will; how is it possible that God should not hear! What petitions wilt Thou, O my God, ever hear (*says St. Augustine*), if Thou dost not hear those which are made after Thy Own heart? "What prayers dost Thou hear, if Thou hearest not these?" (*De Civ. Dei, 1, 22 c. 8*)

But, above all, our confidence ought to revive when we pray to God for spiritual graces, as Jesus Christ says: "If you, being evil, know how to give good gifts to your children, how much more will your Father from Heaven give the good Spirit to them that ask Him!" (*Luke 11: 15*) If you, who are so attached to your own interests, so full of self-love, cannot refuse your children that which they ask, how much more will your Heavenly Father, Who loves you better than any earthly father, grant you His spiritual goods when you pray for them!

4
The perseverance required in prayer

Our prayers, then, must be humble and confident, but this is not enough to obtain final perseverance and thereby eternal life. Individual prayers will obtain the individual graces which they ask of God, but unless they are persevering, they will not obtain final perseverance which, as it is the accumulation of many graces, requires many prayers that are not to cease till death. The grace of salvation is not a single grace, but a chain of graces, all of which are at last linked with the grace of final perseverance. Now, to this chain of graces there ought to correspond another chain (as it were) of our prayers; if we, by neglecting to pray, break the chain of our prayers, the chain of graces will be broken too; and as it is by this that we have to obtain salvation, we shall not be saved.

It is true that we cannot merit final perseverance, as the Council of Trent teaches: "It cannot be had from any other source but from Him Who is able to confirm the man who is standing, that he may stand with perseverance" (*Sess. 6, c. 13*). Nevertheless, says St. Augustine, this great gift of perseverance can in a manner be merited by our prayers; that is, can be obtained by praying: "This gift, therefore, can be suppliantly merited, that is, can be obtained by supplication." And F. Suarez adds that the man who prays, infallibly obtains it. But to obtain it, and to save ourselves, says St. Thomas, a persevering and continual prayer is necessary:

"After Baptism continual prayer is necessary to a man in order that he may enter Heaven" (*P. 3, q. 39, a. 5*). And before this, our Saviour Himself had said it over and over again: "We ought always to pray, and not to faint" (*Luke 18: 1*). "Watch ye therefore, praying at all times, that you may be accounted worthy to escape all these things that are to come, and to stand before the Son of man" (*Luke 21: 36*).

The same had been previously said in the Old Testament: "Let nothing hinder thee from praying always" (*Ecclus. 18: 22*). "Bless God at all times, and desire Him to direct thy ways" (*Job 4: 20*). Hence the Apostle inculcated on his disciples never to neglect prayer: "Pray without intermission" (*1 Thess. 5: 17*). "Be instant in prayer, watching in it with thanksgiving" (*Col. 4: 12*). "I will therefore that men pray in every place" (*1 Tim. 2, 8*). God does indeed wish to give us perseverance, says St. Nilus, but He will only give it to him who prays for it perseveringly: "He willeth to confer benefits on him who perseveres in prayer." Many sinners by the help of God's grace come to be converted and to receive pardon. But then, because they neglect to ask for perseverance, they fall again, and lose all.

Nor is it enough, says Bellarmine, to ask the grace of perseverance once, or a few times; we ought always to ask it, every day till our death, if we wish to obtain it: "It must be asked day by day, that it may be obtained day by day." He who asks it one day, obtains it for that one day; but if he does not ask it the next day, the next day he will fall.

And this is the lesson which our Lord wished to teach us in the parable of the man who would not give his loaves to his friend who asked him for them until he had become importunate in his demand: "Although he will not rise and give because he is his friend, yet because of his importunity, he will rise and give him as many as he needeth" (*Luke 11: 8*). Now if this man, solely to deliver himself from the troublesome importunity of his friend, gave him even against his own will the loaves for which he asked, "how much more," says St. Augustine, "will the good God give, who both commands us to ask, and is angry if we ask not!" (*Serm. 61, E.B.*) How much more will God, Who, as He is infinite goodness, has a commensurate desire to communicate to us His good things,—how much more will He give His graces when we ask Him for them! And the more, as He Himself tells us to ask for them, and as He is displeased when we do not demand them. God, then, does indeed wish to give us eternal life, and therein all graces; but He wishes also that we should never omit to ask Him for them, even to the extent of being troublesome.

Cornelius a Lapide says on the text just quoted, "God wishes us to be persevering in prayer to the extent of importunity."

Men of the world cannot bear the importunate; but God not only bears with them, but wishes us to be importunate in praying to Him for graces, and especially for perseverance. St. Gregory says that God wishes us to do Him violence by our prayers, for such violence does not annoy but pleases Him: "God wills to be called upon, He wills to be forced, He wills to be conquered by importunity... Happy violence, by which God is not offended, but appeased!"

So that to obtain perseverance we must always recommend ourselves to God morning and night, at meditation, at Mass, at Communion, and always; especially in time of temptation, when we must keep repeating, Lord help me; Lord, assist me; keep Thy hand upon me; leave me not; have pity upon me! Is there anything easier than to say, Lord, help me, assist me! The Psalmist says, "With me is prayer to the God of my life" (*Ps. 41: 9*).

On which the gloss is as follows: "A man may say, I cannot fast, I cannot give alms; but if he is told to pray, he cannot say this." Because there is nothing easier than to pray. But we must never cease praying; we must (so to speak) continually do violence to God, that He may assist us always—a violence which is delightful and dear to Him. "This violence is grateful to God," says Tertullian; and St. Jerome says that the more persevering and importunate our prayers are, so much the more are they acceptable to God: "Prayer, as long as it is importunate, is more acceptable."

"Blessed is the man that heareth Me, and that watcheth daily at My gates" (*Prov. 8: 34*). Happy is that man, says God, who listens to Me, and watches continually with holy prayers at the gates of My mercy. And Isaias says, "Blessed are all they that wait for Him" (*Is. 30: 18*). Blessed are they who till the end wait (in prayer) for their salvation from God. Therefore in the

Gospel Jesus Christ exhorts us to pray; but how? "Ask, and ye shall receive; seek, and ye shall find; knock, and it shall be opened to you" (*Luke 11: 9*). Would it not have been enough to have said, "ask?" why add "seek" and "knock?" No, it was not superfluous to add them, for thereby our Saviour wished us to understand that we ought to do as the poor who go begging. If they do not receive the alms they ask (I speak of licensed beggars), they do not cease asking: they return to ask again; and if the master of the house does not show himself any more, they set to work to knock at the door till they become very importunate and troublesome.

That is what God wishes us to do: to pray, and to pray again, and never leave off praying, that He would assist us and succour us, that He would enlighten us and strengthen us, and never allow us to forfeit His grace. The learned Lessius says that the man cannot be excused from mortal sin who does not pray when he is in sin, or in danger of death; or, again, if he neglects to pray for any notable time, as (he says) for one or two months. But this does not include the time of temptations; because whoever finds himself assailed by any grievous temptation, without doubt sins mortally if he does not have recourse to God in prayer, to ask for assistance to resist it; seeing that otherwise he places himself in a proximate, nay, in a certain, occasion of sin.

Why God delays granting us final perseverance. Conclusion.

But, someone will say: Since God can give and wishes to give me the grace of perseverance, why does He not give it me all at once when I ask Him?

The holy Fathers assign many reasons:

(1) God does not grant it at once, but delays it, first, that He may better prove our confidence.

(2) And, further, says St. Augustine, that we may long for it more vehemently. Great gifts, he says, should be greatly desired; for good things soon obtained are not held in the same estimation as those which have been long looked for: "God wills not to give quickly, that you may learn to have great desire for great things; things long desired are pleasanter to obtain, but things "soon given are cheapened" (*Serm. 61, E.B.*).

(3) Again, the Lord does so that we may not forget Him; if we were already secure of persevering and of being saved, and if we had not continual need of God's help to preserve us in His grace and to save us, we should soon forget God. Want makes the poor to keep resorting to the houses of the rich; so God, to draw us to Himself, as St. Chrysostom says, and to see us often at His feet, in order that He may thus be able to do us greater good, delays giving us the complete grace of salvation till the hour of our death: "It is not because He rejects our prayers that He delays, but by this contrivance He wishes to make us careful and to draw us to Himself." Again, He does so in order that we, by persevering in prayer, may unite ourselves closer to Him with the sweet bonds of love: "Prayer," says the same St. Chrysostom, "which is accustomed to converse with God, is no slight bond of love to Him." This continual recurrence to God in prayer, and this confident expectation of the graces which we desire from Him, oh, what a great spur and chain is it of love to inflame us and to bind us more closely to God!

But, till what time have we to pray? Always, says the same Saint, till we receive favourable sentence of eternal life; that is to say, till our death: "Do not leave off till you receive." And he goes on to say that the man who resolves: I will never leave off praying till I am saved, will most certainly be saved: "If you say, I will not give in till I have received, you will assuredly receive."

The Apostle writes that many run for the prize, but that he only receives it who runs till he wins: "Know you not that they who run in the race, all run indeed, but one receiveth the prize? So run that you may obtain" (*1 Cor. 9: 24*). It is not, then, enough for salvation simply to pray, but we must pray always, that we may come to receive the crown which God promises but promises only to those who are constant in prayer till the end.

So that if we wish to be saved, we must do as David did, who always kept his eyes turned to God, to implore His aid against being overcome by his enemies: "My eyes are ever towards the Lord, for He shall pluck my feet out of the snare" (*Ps. 24: 15*). As the devil does not cease continually spreading snares to swallow us up, as St. Peter writes: "Your adversary the devil, as a roaring lion, goeth about, seeking whom he may devour;" (*1 Peter 5*) so ought we ever to stand with our arms in our hands to defend ourselves from such a foe, and to say, with the royal prophet, "I will pursue after my enemies; and I will not turn again till they are consumed" (*Ps. 17: 38*). I will never cease fighting till I see my enemies conquered.

But how can we obtain this victory, so important for us, and so difficult? "By most persevering prayers," says St. Augustine,—only by prayers, and those most persevering; and till when? As long as the fight shall last. "As the battle is never over," says St. Bonaventure, "so let us never give over asking for mercy." As we must be always in the combat, so should we be always asking God for aid not to be overcome. Woe, says the Wise Man, to him who in this battle leaves off praying: "Woe to them that have lost patience" (*Ecclus 2: 16*). We may be saved, the Apostle tells us, but on this condition, "if we retain a firm confidence and the glory of hope until the end" (*Heb. 3: 6*), if we are constant in praying with confidence until death.

Let us, then, take courage from the mercy of God, and His promises, and say with the same Apostle, "Who then shall separate us from the love of Christ? Shall tribulation, or distress, or danger or persecution, or the sword?" (*Rom. 8: 35, 37*) Who shall succeed in estranging us from the love of Jesus Christ? Tribulation, perhaps, or the danger of losing the goods of this world? The persecutions of devils or men? The torments inflicted by tyrants? "In all these we overcome," (it is St. Paul who encourages us), "because of Him that hath loved us" (*Ibid*). No, he says, no tribulation, no misery, danger, persecution, or torture, shall ever be able to separate us from the love of Jesus Christ, because with God's help we shall overcome all, if we fight for love of Him who gave his life for us.

F. Hippolitus Durazzo, the day when he resolved to relinquish his dignity of prelate at Rome and to give himself entirely to God by entering the Society of Jesus (which he afterwards did), was so afraid of being faithless by reason of his weakness that he said to God, "Forsake me not, Lord, now that I have given myself wholly to Thee; for pity's sake, do not forsake me!" But he heard the whisper of God in his heart, "Do not thou forsake Me; rather," said God, "do I say to thee, forsake Me not." And so at last the servant of God, trusting in His goodness and help, concluded, "Then, O my God, Thou wilt not leave me, and I will not leave Thee."

Finally, if we wish not to be forsaken by God, we ought never to forsake praying to Him not to leave us. If we do thus, He will certainly always assist us, and will never allow us to perish and to be separated from His love. And to this end let us not only take care always to ask for final perseverance and the graces necessary to obtain it, but let us, at the same time, always by anticipation ask God for grace to go on praying; for this is precisely that great gift which He promised to His elect by the mouth of the prophet: "And I will pour out upon the house of David, and upon the inhabitants of Jerusalem, the spirit of grace and prayers" (*Zach. 12: 10*).

Oh, what a great grace is the spirit of prayer; that is, the grace which God confers on a soul to enable it to pray always! Let us, then, never neglect to beg God to give us this grace and this spirit of continual prayer; because if we pray always, we shall certainly obtain from God perseverance and every other gift which we desire, since His promise of hearing whoever prays to Him cannot fail. "For we are saved by hope" (*Rom. 8: 24*). With this hope of always praying, we may reckon ourselves saved. "Confidence will give us a broad entrance into this city." This hope, said Venerable Bede, will give us a safe passage into the city of Paradise.

www.ingramcontent.com/pod-product-compliance
Lightning Source LLC
Chambersburg PA
CBHW030303010526
44107CB00053B/1794